OOP CONCEPTS BOOSTER

TAKE YOUR
CODING SKILLS
TO THE NEXT LEVEL

RAKESH SINGH

INDIA · SINGAPORE · MALAYSIA

Notion Press

Old No. 38, New No. 6
McNichols Road, Chetpet
Chennai - 600 031

First Published by Notion Press 2019
Copyright © Rakesh Singh 2019
All Rights Reserved.

ISBN 978-1-64733-680-6

Contents

Quick Notes

OOP Questions

Puspa Lamichhane

BTech, being in an editor role, she made sure that the content of this book is in a specific order for easy understanding. In fact, while writing this book, she has been a testing instrument to make sure the book's content is simple to grasp. Unquestionably, her object-oriented programming skill is enhanced as a result of this process. -Author

What she says,

Simply, this is an amazing book to leverage the OOP concepts and enhance coding skills. Rakesh has beautifully clarified all the confusing elements of the OOP in a very simple manner that is easy to consume. I loved his dedication to delivering the best for the readers' benefits. He has gone through multiple iterations with various novice programmers to make the answers of complicated and confusing elements simple to consume and that was awesome. I enjoyed the book a lot and it been a great learning experience.

Kuheli Dey

MCA, being in the role of editor, she made sure that each concept and code are accurate and fine-grained. She got an amazing experience and leverages her coding skills during this process. - Author

What she says,

This is an ultimate book to skyrocket the OOP concepts and coding skills. What makes this book special is, the author has made sure that the readers will find the content familiar with their logical concepts, and novice readers get industry-level knowledge. It has been lots of learning and fun.

About the Book

An OOP user faces the given questions in this book day-in and day-out. Each of these questions poses multiple options to the OOP user. The rationale for choosing an option requires the crystal-clear perception of the effects of exercising the option. The content of the book is an attempt to build such clarity in the mind of the OOP user, that helps leverage his OOP concepts & coding skills to effectively build high-quality software.

The book contains notes with important points on various OOP concepts for quick revision and 25 fine blended questions on the concepts with detailed answers and code examples. It isn't an OOAD (object-oriented analysis and design) book, however, you'll get a flavor of it.

The book does not address the basics such as loops and conditions etc. or techniques that use oops such as exceptions, serialization, etc. but rather focuses on boosting the concept of oop. However, you can search and read the topics of your choice on the site https://www.interviewsansar.com.

The code samples are illustrated using Java language. Nevertheless, the treatment of the oop concepts by this book is language agnostic, hence C++ and C#, etc. are also equally and fully suitable for illustration.

Here's how this book helps readers:

- ✓ Clarity on OOP nuances.

- ✓ Learn to use OOP concepts to effectively build high-quality software.

- ✓ Focused on WHY and HOW of using the OOP concepts, rather than WHAT.

- ✓ Write more maintainable and flexible code by adapting different OOP features.

- ✓ Enables COLLEGE students and FRESHERS to get industry-level knowledge in no time.

- ✓ Makes JOB SEEKER interviews surprisingly impressive.

Why is this book produced?

There are primarily three reasons to produce this book that are stated below. Besides this, it is observed that many programmers lose focus on utilizing the powerful features of the OOP in a project somehow, even though they are excellent at the concepts. Some of the programmers get confusion in utilizing the concepts. This is where it is written to make them focus and build clarity on object-oriented programming concepts.

A decade ago, I lost a million-dollar project because my team and I skipped incorporating the amazing features of the OOP concept resulting in a rigid & bad code structure.

Initially, from scratch, we built a gaming project but didn't focus on the powerful features of OOP. Somehow, we released the first build successfully. Now, the maintenance starts, and for multiple upcoming releases, the team started spending hectic days and nights with huge frustration because of the bad code structure.

The client asked the team to make a simple extension within a week, only then the project will be extended for the coming years. But, as per the estimation of efforts and time, we're ready to give it in three months.

That's where we lost the project.

This was a great pain to me, and I was terribly hurt.

I wanted to learn from the lesson. So, I analyzed if it were doable within a weak. The analysis took me a month besides my other task.

Surprisingly, I found that we didn't use the OOP concepts effectively in the project resulting in the bad code structure causing difficulties in maintaining and extending features. I researched on OOP concepts more for months and realized that the project extension could have been done within a week.

This incident changed my way of coding and designing the system. It changed my mindset towards writing flexible and maintainable design and code producing quality software. As a start, the first simple step I took was, simply focusing on **why and how to use** coop concepts effectively and learn many things.

Since then, I worked on multiple projects, refactored, re-design and developed the software and can see the improved differences in my efforts and time maintaining and extending features of an application.

Secondly, when I started training college students, who know the very basics of the OOP concept. They were very curious to know why the OOP paradigm such as encapsulation, abstract, inheritance, and interfaces, etc. are used and how to use them in a program. They wanted to get the industry level knowledge in fact.

Third, I came across multiple job seekers complaining that they were well versed in OOP and coding, but still not getting a job. When I took their mock interviews, I came to know that, they were missing the knowledge matching to the industry's requirements. When I trained them, they cracked the interviews easily and got a job in a shorter period of time.

That's where I thought to write this OOP concept booster in the form of questions & answers format with quick notes.

Quick Notes

A class is a template or blueprint that contains properties and behaviours of an object that can be used to create multiple objects with **similar** properties and behaviours.

[Properties are known as class fields or class member variables, and behaviours are known as class methods.]

For example,

a person has certain properties and behaviours. A person has his name, age, gender, etc. as a property, and behaviours like eating and sleeping, etc.

Here is the representation of the class for the given example.

```java
class Person {
    // properties
    private String name;
    private int age;

    // Behaviors
    public void eat() {

    }

    public void sleep() {

    }
}
```

We have created a template class for a person. Now, we can create many objects of the *Person* class.

Person peter = **new** Person();

Person john = **new** Person();

Objects can be any person e.g. peter, john and linda and so on. Everyone has their own properties such as name and age and similar behaviours such as eating and sleeping etc.

Note that, in the statement `Person peter = new Person();`,

the *"new Person();"* statement creates an object at run time and the reference of it is assigned to the reference variable *peter*.

If you need to call only one method of the object in a program, you can create a class object without a reference variable and invoke the method as shown below.

```
public class Sample {

    public static void main(String[] args) {

        new Person().eat();
    }
}
```

If you want to call **multiple methods on the same object**, then you need a reference variable as shown in the following sample code (the *peter* is a reference variable that references the object of the *Person* class).

```java
public class Sample {

    public static void main(String[] args) {

        Person peter = new Person();
        peter.eat();
        peter.sleep();
    }
}
```

NOTE

*In the statements **new** Person().eat(); and **new** Person().sleep(); , both the eat() and sleep() methods respectively are called on **different objects**.*

Typically, we use a direct object such as **new** *Person()*, when we need to pass an object to a method. In the given example, in the *main()* method, we are passing a direct object of the *Person* class to the *dine* method of the *Restaurant* class.

```java
class Restaurant {

    public void dine(Person p) {
        p.eat();
    }
}

public class Sample {

    public static void main(String[] args) {

        Restaurant r = new Restaurant();
        r.dine(new Person());

    }
}
```

Also, we can use a direct object statement to call a single method on an object as shown below.

```
new Person().eat();
```

ADDITIONAL NOTE

As a best practice in class design, always declare member variables private unless required. You can provide access to it from the outside of the class using a public method as shown in the below class Person.

The primary benefits are,

I) It prevents changing the values of the variables from outside accidentally.

II) It also helps maintain a program easily.

Consider, if a class variable is public, it can be **directly accessed** (without using a method) from multiple places across a program. At a later point in time, if you decide to change the variable name for some reason (*maybe naming convention changed requirement for example*), at all the places where it has been used directly, compile-time errors will be thrown, and you need to put effort correcting and maintaining them.

If the variable is private and you have provided its access via a public method, changing the class variable name will not affect the program.

```
class Person {

        private String name;
        private int age;

        public String getName() {
                return name;
        }

        public int getAge() {
                return age;
        }

        public void eat() {

        }

        public void sleep() {

        }
}
```

Important points about a method of a class

I) A return type of a method

a) A method of a class **must have a return type**. If the method does not return anything, then declare the return type as **void**. For example, the findJobs() method does not return anything, so the return type is void.

```
        private void findJobs() {
                this.count = 100;
        }
```

b) A method can also return a class data type. For example, in the code example given below, the *jobCount()* method of the *Job* class is returning an object of the *Search* class, hence the return type of the method is of *Search* class type.

```java
class Job {

        // Return number of jobs
        public Search jobCount() {

                return new Search();
        }
}

class Search {
        private int count;

        public int getCount() {

                findJobs();

                return count;
        }

        private void findJobs() {
                this.count = 100;
        }
}
```

II) Method parameters Vs Arguments:

Parameters: When we declare a method and declare variables inside the parenthesis, then it is known as method parameters.

```java
public int sum(int a, int b)
```

Arguments: The values received in method parameters from a method calling point in the program are known as arguments.

III) A static method of a class is called using the class name only and object creation of the class is not required. For example, the *sleep()* method of the *Person* class is static and has only been invoked with the name of the class *Person*.

```java
class Person {

    public static void sleep() {

    }
}

public class Sample {

    public static void main(String[] args) {

        Person.sleep();
    }
}
```

Constructor

A constructor of a class is a special method that has the **same name as the class name.**

```
class Person {
        // Constructor
        public Person() {


        }
}
```

The constructor is primarily used to initialize the class fields with default values.

```
class Person {
        private String name;

        // Constructor
        public Person() {

                this.name = "Peter"; // initialize the name
field
        }
}
```

The constructor is **automatically** called when you create an object of the class. For example, on creating an object e.g. *"new Person ();"* the constructor will be called automatically.

A class can have multiple constructors with different numbers of parameters as shown below.

```
class Person {
        String name;
        // Constructor
        public Person() {

                this.name = "Peter"; // initialize the name field
        }

        public Person(String name) {
                this.name = name; // initialize the field explic-
itly
        }
}
```

When we create a class object with or without arguments, the matching class constructor is called. For example,

```
Person peter = new Person ();
Person john = new Person("John");
```

The *peter* object will call the empty parameter constructor *Person ().*

The *john* object will call the parameterized constructor *Person (String name)* of the class.

If you don't write any constructors in the class, the compiler will provide the constructor internally by default. If you create one, the compiler will not provide the default one.

The class constructor does not have a return type because it is not intended to return a value but to initialize an object (class fields).

In the parent-child relationship in inheritance, the first parent class constructor and then the child class constructor will be executed when you create the child class object. So, the order of constructor execution is from parent to child.

```
class Person {

    // Constructor
    public Person() {

    }
}

class Employee extends Person {

    public Employee() {

    }
}
```

NOTE

An empty constructor of a class is generally used to initialize class fields with default values implicitly.

A parameterized constructor is used to initialize class fields with default values explicitly.

Inheritance

Inheritance is a mechanism in which a class can access fields and methods of another class. It forms a parent and child relationship.

✓ *A parent class is also called as a base or a super class.*

✓ *A child class is also known as a derived class or a subclass.*

If you want to re-use the functionality already implemented in an existing class, you can use inheritance that saves time and effort by re-writing and testing it again.

For example, the below *MediaPlayer* class has access to the *Player* class features i.e. *play, pause, stop* and *codec* by inheriting it.

```java
//Base class
class Player {
      public void play() {
      }

      public void pause() {
      }

      public void stop() {
      }

      public void codec() {
      }
}


// Child class
class MediaPlayer extends Player {

      public void files() {
      }
}
```

You can access all public methods of the *Player* class using the *MediaPlayer* Class object as shown below.

```java
public class Sample {

      public static void main(String[] args) {

            MediaPlayer mp = new MediaPlayer();
            mp.files();
            mp.codec();
            mp.play();
            mp.pause();
            mp.stop();
      }
}
```

It should be noted that the private methods of a parent class will not be available to the child classes.

Also, private variables are not accessible directly to the child class, however the access of the private variables can be provided via public methods.

In the example, the private variable *playlistId* is accessible via public methods *getPlaylistId()* and *setPlaylistId(int playlistId)*.

```
// Child class
class MediaPlayer extends Player {
    private int playlistId;

    public int getPlaylistId() {
        return playlistId;
    }

    public void setPlaylistId(int playlistId) {
        this.playlistId = playlistId;
    }

    public void files() {
    }
}
```

Inheritance can be used with an abstract class and **interfaces** besides normal classes.

Inheritance with an interface:

The abstract methods of **interfaces** are inherited and implemented by the classes. The *Tablet* class has inherited and implemented the *charge ()* abstract method of the interface *Charger*.

```java
interface Charger {
     void charge(); // By default abstract, static &
public
}


class Tablet implements Charger {

     @Override
     public void charge() {
     }
}
```

Inheritance with an abstract class:

The defined methods and abstract methods of an **abstract class** are inherited by the classes. A class can use the defined method or override it and give its own definition. The class will implement the abstract methods.

In the given example, the *Coffee* class is inheriting and using the *addMilk()* defined method of the *Beverages* abstract class and has overridden and implemented the *addIngredient()* method.

```java
abstract class Beverages {
     // Defined
     public void addMilk() {

     }
     // abstract
     abstract void addIngredient();
}


class Coffee extends Beverages {

     void addIngredient() {
     }
}
```

Depending on the need, the *Coffee* class can override the *addMilk()* method and give its own definition as below.

```
class Coffee extends Beverages {

    @Override
    public void addMilk() {

    }

    @Override
    void addIngredient() {

    }
}
```

TYPES OF INHERITANCE

There are different types of inheritance techniques that can be used in object-oriented programming as given below.

1. Single Inheritance

2. Multilevel Inheritance

3. Hierarchical Inheritance

4. Hybrid inheritance

5. Multiple Inheritance

Single Inheritance:

It's just a one-level parent and child class relationship There should be only one base class and its child classes. The example of a media player you've already seen.

Multilevel Inheritance:

In Multilevel inheritance, a class is derived from another class, which is also derived from another class.

For example, The *Son* class is derived from the *Father* class and the *Father* class is derived from the *Person* class as shown in the following example.

```
class Person {

    public void eat() {

    }

    public void sleep() {

    }
}

class Father extends Person {

    public void useCar() {

    }
}

class Son extends Father {

    public void useMobile() {

    }
}
```

Hierarchical Inheritance:

In a hierarchical inheritance, more than one subclass inherits the same class. In the example above, both the *Son* class and the *Daughter* class can inherit the *Father* class forming hierarchical inheritance.

```java
class Son extends Father {

    public void useMobile() {

    }
}

class Daughter extends Father {

    public void useMobile() {

    }
}
```

Hybrid inheritance:

In hybrid inheritance, we use a mixture of different types of inheritance relationships. For example, we can mix multi-level and hierarchical inheritance.

Examples given in a multi-level and hierarchical inheritance will produce a hybrid inheritance if you combine them as shown below in the code example.

```java
class Person {

    public void eat() {

    }

    public void sleep() {

    }
}

class Father extends Person {

    public void useCar() {

    }
}

class Son extends Father {

    public void useMobile() {

    }
}

class Daughter extends Father {

    public void useMobile() {

    }
}
```

Multiple Inheritance:

Java and C# like languages do not support multiple inheritance. You cannot inherit more than one class like C++. This is by design and not given support in the framework.

However, you can inherit methods of multiple interfaces and implement them in classes as shown in the given example.

```
interface Flyable {
     void fly();
}

interface Edible {
     void eat();
}
```

The *fly()* and *eat()* methods of *Flyable* interface and *Edible* interface respectively are inherited and implemented by the *Bird* class.

```
class Bird implements Flyable, Edible {

     public void fly() {
          System.out.println("Bird flying");
     }

     public void eat() {
          System.out.println("Bird eats");
     }
     // It can have more own methods.
}
```

Polymorphism

Polymorphism implies many forms. The same function (behaviour) can have different forms.

A function can have different forms in a class. e.g. a screen can have a display functionality and it can have many forms as shown below with different parameters.

```
void display(String text)
void display(String text, Image img)
void display(Image img)
```

A class constructor can have different forms with different numbers of parameters to initialize class fields with default values, e.g. a *Car* class can have many constructors.

```
Car(String model)
Car(String model, double price)
```

Similarly, the parent and child class can also have methods with the same name, the implementation of which can be class-specific.

We can say that,

Polymorphism = Same behaviour with different implementations.

Polymorphism can be implemented by the following techniques in OOP:

- ✓ Constructor overloading
- ✓ Method overloading
- ✓ Method overriding

Let's have a look at each technique one by one.

Constructor Overloading

Writing multiple constructors within a class, **either** with a different number of parameters **or** with different data types of parameters, when the number of parameters is the same, is known as overloading constructors.

```
class Car {
        // Empty constructor
        public Car() {
        }

        // Constructor with 1 parameter
        public Car(String model) {
        }

        // Constructor with 2 parameters
        public Car(String model, double price) {
        }

        // Constructors with same number of parameters
        public Car(int count) {

        }

        public Car(double price) {

        }
}
```

When you create an object of the class, then the matching constructor will be called automatically. It should be noted that the same matching constructor will be called as many times as you create an object of the class.

The statement *Car x = new Car("Swift");* will call the *"public Car (String model)"* constructor.

The statement *Car x = new Car ("Swift", 500000);* will call the *"public Car (String model, double price)"* constructor.

Method Overloading

Having multiple methods with the same name having different numbers of parameters or different data types if the number of parameters is the same within a class is known as Method overloading. It is also known as compile-time polymorphism as the methods get resolved at compile time itself.

The below *Screen* class has a *display* functionality with different inputs and implementations.

```
class Screen {

    public void display(String text) {
        // Display only text
    }

    public void display(Image img) {
        // Display only image
    }

    public void display(String text, Image img) {
        // Display text with image
    }
}
```

Methods are typically overloaded **within a class** for variants of the same behaviour. For instance, the behaviour of all the *display* methods of the *Screen* class is the same, i.e. display data, but with different inputs.

Method Overriding

In method overriding, both the parent and child contain methods with the same name and signature.

In the following example, the Son wanted to use his own car, not the Father's car, so he overrides the method and defines it on his own. The daughter wanted to keep using her father's car, so she didn't override it.

Both the *Father* class and the *Son* class have a method with the same name i.e. *useCar()*.

```
class Father {

    public void useCar() {
    }
}

class Son extends Father {

    public void useCar() {
    }
}

class daughter extends Father {

}
```

A method of an interface is overridden by the classes who implement it. e.g. the *Screen* interface has deferred/enforced implementation of *setLCD()* method to the *TV* class.

The interface *Screen* and *TV* class both have a method with the same name.

```java
interface Screen {
    void setLCD();
}


class TV implements Screen {
    @Override
    public void setLCD() {
        System.out.println("TV has LCD Screen");
    }
}
```

Similarly, an abstract class' defined method and abstract methods can also be overridden by subclasses.

The *addIngredient()* method is overridden by the *Coffee* class.

```java
abstract class Beverages {

    // Defined
    public void addMilk() {

    }

    // abstract
    abstract void addIngredient();
}


class Coffee extends Beverages {

    void addIngredient() {
        System.out.println("add Coffee");
    }
}
```

NOTE

The overloading of the constructor and the overloading of the method can only be done within a class, whereas the method overriding is always applicable to the parent and child relationship, whatever, class and subclasses, an interface and subclasses or an abstract class and subclasses.

Polymorphic implementation means the execution of a method is decided by **the sub-class object being referenced by the base reference** at runtime. You can read details with an example in the answer to question #6.

Interface

An interface defines certain specifications (abstract methods) that **must** be implemented by the classes who use the interface.

```
interface Charger {
    void charge(); // By default abstract
}
```

By default, all methods in the interface are public and abstract.

An interface forces you to **define all its specifications (abstract methods)** when you create a class and implement the interface.

```
class Mobile implements Charger {

    @Override
    public void charge() {

    }
}
```

It should be noted that if you implement the interface in a class, you **must** define all the abstract methods of the interface. If you leave any method undefined in the class, the compiler will display an error.

This is how we use a class that implements an interface.

```
public class Sample {

    public static void main (String [] args) {

        Mobile m = new Mobile ();
        m.charge();
    }
}
```

You cannot create an object of an interface. However, it can be used as a reference variable that refers to its subclasses' object as shown in the code example.

```
public class Sample {

    public static void main(String[] args) {

        // interface reference with class object
        Charger m = new Mobile();
        m.charge();
    }
}
```

An interface can extend another interface

```
interface A {
    void fa();
}


interface B extends A {
    void fb();
}
```

The class can implement either the *A* interface or the *B* interface. If the class only needs to define the method *fa*, interface *A* will be used. If both methods are needed, implements the interface *B*.

Multiple interfaces can be implemented by a class at the same time

We have two interfaces the Flyable and Edible that will be implemented by the class Bird.

```
interface Flyable {
     void fly();
}


interface Edible {
     void eat();
}
```

The Bird class is implementing the both interfaces. Notice the declaration syntax for both interfaces.

```
// Bird class has implemented both the interfaces
class Bird implements Flyable, Edible {

     public void fly() {
          System.out.println("Bird flying");
     }

     public void eat() {
          System.out.println("Bird eats");
     }
     // It can have more own methods.
}
```

An interface can contain variables

An interface can contain variables. By default, the variables in an interface are public, static, and final.

Typically, we keep collections of related constants in an interface.

```
interface Math {
    public static final double     PI = 3.14;
    public static final double ELUERNUMBER = 2.718;
    public static final double SQRT = 1.41421;
}
```

You can access the interface variables such as *Math.PI* and *Math. SQRT* etc. into a program.

Abstract method

A method that has only a declaration and no implementation (no body) is known as an abstract method. The abstract methods are used in an interface or an abstract class as shown below.

```
interface Charger {
    void charge(); // By default abstract
}


abstract class Beverages {

    abstract void addIngredient();
}
```

Abstract methods are designed to be implemented by subclasses that extend the abstract class or implement the interface.

Extending the abstract class

```
class Tea extends Beverages{

    @Override
    void addIngredient() {
        // Do Something
    }
}
```

Implementing the interface

```
class Mobile implements Charger {

    @Override
    public void charge() {

    }
}
```

In fact, an abstract method in an interface or an abstract class is used to enforce subclasses to implement (override and define) it.

Abstract class

The abstract class is designed to include both defined and abstract methods. This class may contain only defined methods or abstract methods or both.

```
abstract class Beverages {

    // Defined
    public void addMilk() {

    }

    // abstract
    abstract void addIngredient();
}
```

NOTE

An abstract class may not contain an abstract method. But, if an abstract method is present in the class, the class must be declared abstract.

Subclasses may extend the abstract class, use its defined methods and implement abstract methods. Below, the *Coffee* subclass is using the *addMilk()* method of the *Beverages* abstract class and have implemented the abstract method *addIngredient()*.

```
class Coffee extends Beverages {

        void addIngredient() {
                System.out.println("add Coffee");
        }
}
```

Sample to use the Coffee class:

```
public class Sample {

        public static void main(String[] args) {

                Coffee b = new Coffee();
                b.addMilk();
                b.addIngredient();

        }
}
```

It should be noted that the **object of an abstract class cannot be created**. However, it can be used as a reference variable to store reference of a Subclass as given below.

```
public class Sample {

        public static void main(String[] args) {

                // abstract class reference and subclass
object
                Beverages b = new Coffee();
                b.addMilk();
                b.addIngredient();

        }
}
```

Some Important Points:

An abstract class can extend another class. The *Truck* abstract class has extended the *Vehicle* class in the example given below.

```
class Vehicle{
      public void start(){

      }
      public void stop(){

      }
}

abstract class Truck extends Vehicle {

public abstract void run();

      public void carry() {

      }
}
```

The class who extends the Truck abstract class will also have access to methods of the Vehicle class.

The following MiniTruck subclass has extended the abstract class Truck, also has access to the Vehicle class methods in addition to the abstract class methods.

```java
class MiniTruck extends Truck {

    @Override
    public void run() {

    }
}
```

Below is a sample, that demonstrate the methods invocation of the Vehicle, Truck and MiniTruck classes.

```java
public class Sample {

    public static void main(String[] args) {

        MiniTruck mt = new MiniTruck();
        mt.start();
        mt.stop();
        mt.carry();
        mt.run();
    }
}
```

An abstract class can implement an interface as shown here.

```java
interface Chargeable {

    void charge();
}

abstract class Truck implements Chargeable {

    public abstract void run();

    public void carry() {

    }
}
```

The subclass who extends the abstract class must implement the abstract methods of both the interface and abstract class as well.

```
class MiniTruck extends Truck {

    @Override
    public void charge() {

    }

    @Override
    public void run() {

    }
}
```

Also, note that you can override and define (implement) the abstract methods of the interface in the **abstract class itself**.

In the below example, the abstract class *Truck* has overridden and defined the method *charge ()* of the *Chargeable* interface.

```
interface Chargeable {

    void charge();
}

abstract class Truck implements Chargeable {

    public abstract void run();

    public void carry() {

    }

    public void charge() {
    }
}
```

An abstract class can have a constructor. When we create an object of the subclass, the constructor will be invoked automatically. If the abstract class contains fields, they can be initialized with default values or if we want to perform some operations (methods) before creating an object of the subclass, then it helps.

Abstraction & Encapsulation

Definition:

Encapsulation says to hide complexities and internal implementation details from a client(user).

Abstraction says to expose only essential details to the users.

You can design a class that is well encapsulated and abstracted from the users e.g. another class, part of the program, etc. who use the designed class.

Abstraction is a design level concept in which you decide what needs to be provided or what part of the code to be exposed to a user for his better experience.

Whereas, the encapsulation is an implementation level concept, in which you hide complexities, data and internal implementation details from the client. Whatever, you think, need to be hidden from the user, you encapsulate that.

Come back here after reading the answer of question #14 to get a crystal-clear picture that details the abstraction and encapsulation with code examples and differences.

Keep this in mind that,

"The abstraction can be achieved through encapsulation, interface and an abstract class."

When you use encapsulation, it automatically provides abstraction. In other words, encapsulation implements abstraction.

Read the answer to question #19 to see how an interface and abstract class are used to achieve abstraction.

NOTE

Many novice programmers think that the definition of encapsulation is, wrapping a class variable into a method. That's it.

In fact, this is merely an example of the encapsulation and this definition does not communicate the encapsulation in fact. A class itself is an example of encapsulation. You hide or prevent methods from users or client code by making them private, this is also an example of encapsulation.

Hence, hide complexities and internal implementation details from a client(user) suits best to the encapsulation definition.

The Author Simon Kendal in his book object-oriented programming using C# says the following about the encapsulation and abstraction.

Encapsulation allows us to focus on what something does without considering the complexities of how it works.

Abstraction allows us to consider complex ideas while ignoring irrelevant detail that would confuse us.

In other words,

Encapsulation allows us to hide the complexities and inner details and focus on what the system does. The complexities should be hidden from a user.

Abstraction allows us to consider only the essential idea/details what is necessary to the users and ignore the irrelevant details. Simply, provide the essential details to the user.

Singleton Class

The Singleton class is not an OOP concept, just it is a technique to create a class which allows users to create a single object only of it throughout the program. To understand some of the answers, you should be aware of it. So, as a reference example, the singleton class is briefed here.

Singleton class restricts a class's instantiation to a single instance and ensures that there is only one instance of the class throughout the application.

Singleton class users, i.e. other classes and methods cannot create an object of the singleton class on their own. But, the singleton class itself creates an object and provides users with the same unique object through a public and static method.

NOTE

The Singleton class is just a concept of design and in any language such as Java, C # or C++ there is no keyword. Depending on your requirements, you can design any class as Singleton.

Steps to create a singleton class

Step – 1) Make the class constructors private, so that the class object cannot be created outside the class.

Step – 2) Create a private static class-type variable as a member field to hold a class object reference. This variable has to be static because it will be used in a static method. The static method can only access the static variable.

Step – 3) Create a static method, e.g. *getInstance()* that returns a class object created in the class itself.

The *getInstance()* method will be static so that the object can be called from outside the class using only the name of the class. Since the user class or method cannot create an object of the singleton class, the object can be accessed using the *getInstance()* method.

Singleton Class Code Example

The *Car* class given below has been designed as a singleton class that returns the same unique instance.

Whenever a user calls the *getInstance()* method, the method will check whether or not the *Car* instance variable is null. If it is null, the object of the *Car* class will be created and returned. If it is not null, the same object that was created before will be returned.

```
class Car {
        private static Car instance;
        // Disallow creating object from outside
        private Car() {
        }

        // Handle single object
        public static Car getInstance() {

                if (instance == null) {
                        instance = new Car();
                }
                return instance;
        }

        public void run() {
        }
}
```

```
public class Sample {

        public static void main(String[] args) {

                Car c1 = Car.getInstance();
                c1.run();

                Car c2 = Car.getInstance();
                c2.run();
        }
}
```

*The getInstance() method will return the **same object on different calls**.*

OOP Questions

Q-1) What are the memory view of the objects and the references of a class? When is the memory allocated to them cleared and who clears this memory? What is the lifespan of the objects and their references?

Answer:

We'll check out at what part of the memory, an object of a class and a variable that references the object resides.

Memory view:

Let's understand it with a *Car* class object example and the memory view image of the class reference and object given below.

```
class Car {
        private int price;
        private String model;

        public void start() {
        }
        public void stop() {
        }
}
```

When we create an object of the *Car* class as below.

```
Car myCar = new Car();
```

Then the *"new Car()"* statement will create an object on the HEAP region of the memory dynamically at the run time. The reference of the object will be assigned to the *myCar* reference variable of the class *Car*. The *myCar* variable is created on the STACK.

At runtime, an object of a class is dynamically created on heap memory which is referenced by a variable resides on the stack.

Reference and Object Memory View

Freeing memory:

Freeing reference variable memory:

You understand that the reference variables reside on the STACK memory. If a reference variable goes out of the scope, it is cleared from the STACK that releases the space.

Freeing object's memory:

The GC (Garbage Collector) residing in the JVM, deletes the object and frees the memory assigned to the object when the object is not referenced anywhere in the program.

In the above example, the memory allocated to the object will be released automatically by GC if the *myCar* reference variable goes out of scope and no other variable holds the reference of the object of the *Car* class.

NOTE

I) In colloquial programmer talk, the above activity is also said as "JVM frees the memory automatically". It is implicit that GC is the actual actor in this activity.

So, we can say that when an object is not referenced by any variable in the program, JVM automatically clears the memory. Programmers do not have the responsibility to delete the object.

II) To explicitly make an object eligible for garbage collection, you can set the null value to the reference variable which is referring to the object.

You know that when a reference variable goes out of scope, the object, it is referring to will be eligible for garbage collection, if not referenced from anywhere else. Consider the given code example below. The scope of the *myCar* reference variable is within the *main()* method. So, the car object will be eligible for garbage collection once the *myCar* variable goes out of scope.

```
public class Sample {
    public static void main(String[] args) {

        Car myCar = new Car();
    }
}
```

But, if you want the object to be eligible for garbage collection before the end of the *main ()* method, then you can set the null value to the *myCar* variable.

```
public class Sample {
    public static void main(String[] args) {

        Car myCar = new Car();
        myCar = null;

        // more Statements
    }
}
```

The lifespan of the objects and their references:

We create multiple objects and reference variables within methods and classes in a program. We pass objects to methods or methods of different objects and store in a reference variable and use those reference variables to invoke methods etc. Don't we?

We'll understand the life span of an object created dynamically at the run time and a reference variable that points to the object in a program using a program example scenario.

But, before example and explanation, let's have a brief of what is the scope and the lifespan of the variables and objects.

Scope of variables:

Scope of a variable means, the section of a code block in which the variable is visible and not accessible outside of the block.

The lifespan of variable and object:

The lifespan of a variable or an object means, how long a variable or an object persists in the program before it is destroyed.

Consider the following program for simple understanding, which includes the *Mobile, User* and *Sample* classes. Read the program description after the code.

```java
class Mobile {

    public void installApp() {
        System.out.println("Install app");
    }

    public void useApp(User john) {
        System.out.println("Use Application");
        john.viewUI();
    }
```

```
        public void buy() {
                User peter = new User();
                peter.viewUI();
        }
}


class User {

        public void viewUI() {
                System.out.println("View App interface");
        }
}


public class Sample {

        public static void main(String[] args) {

                Mobile mi = new Mobile();
                User linda = new User();
                mi.useApp(linda);

        }
}
```

Program Description:

Two objects of the *User* class have been created in the program. The first object, in the *main ()* method of the *Sample* class i.e. *User linda = new User ()* and the second object, in the *buy ()* method of the *Mobile* class i.e. *User peter = new User ();*

Also, one object of the *Mobile* class has been created in the *main ()* method i.e. *Mobile mi = new Mobile ();*

Note that all variables, *linda, peter, mi* are the reference variables of respective classes, as they hold the respective objects references.

The lifespan of reference variables:

The lifespan of the *john* variable is within the *useApp(User john)* method, as it is a parameter variable and its life must be within the method body itself. At the end of the method, the variable, *john* will be removed from stack memory.

The life of the variable *peter* is within the *buy()* method only.

The life of the variable *linda* is within the *main()* method.

The life of the variable *mi* is within the *main()* method only.

The lifespan of Objects:

The lifespan of an object means when an object is eligible for GC (garbage collection).

Let's see the lifespan of the objects created in the given program example.

GC eligibility of the object created in the *buy()* method:

The object of the *User* class created in the *buy ()* method is referenced by only *peter* variable. Since *peter* variable has life within the method *buy()* itself. So, after the end of this method, the object will be eligible for garbage collection.

GC eligibility of the object created in the *main()* method:

The object of *User* class created in the *main ()* method is referenced by the variable *linda*. The object reference is also sent to the *Mobile* class's *useApp(User john)* method, which is copied to the *john* variable.

When the *john* variable gets out of scope, the object is still referenced by the variable *linda*. So, the object will be eligible for garbage collection at the end of the *main()* method.

The *Mobile* class object is referenced by the *mi* variable only and its life is also within the *main ()* method only. Hence, the mobile object will be eligible for garbage collection at the end of the *main ()* method.

NOTE

The good naming convention of a method parameter should be generic like *useApp(User user)*. I wrote *john* e.g. *useApp(User john)* to make the explanation easier for better understanding.

Q-2) What is the effect of a private constructor of a class and in what scenarios can it be beneficial?

Answer:

The effect of a private constructor is that the class cannot be instantiated by any client (classes/programs). The specific scenarios of benefits are: **(I)** Singleton implementation. **(II)** During inheritance, restrict the children, from invoking the private constructor(s).

First, I'll elaborate on the stopping of object creation using a private constructor and then both the scenarios **I & II** mentioned above.

Recommendation: Frist read about the Singleton class with the example under the quick notes section.

Stop object creation of a class using private constructors:

If you want to stop object creation of a class from outside of it, for example, from the main program or other classes, then you can make the class constructors private.

You know that when we create an object of a class from outside, then the matching **public** constructor gets called automatically. If the constructor is private and we create an object from outside, the compiler will flash an error, because the constructor will not be accessible from outside the class as shown here.

```
class Person {
     private String name;

     private Person() {
          this.name = "Peter";
     }
}
```

Following is the test class.

```
public class Sample {

    public static void main(String[] args) {

        Person obj = new Person();// Error
    }
}
```

NOTE

I)To stop object creation of a class completely, you need to make all the overloaded constructors (multiple constructors in the class) private.

II)There may be a chance that you need to stop a specific type of object creation. You can do so by making the specific constructor private.

For example, if you don't want to allow anyone to create an object of a class from outside with an empty constrictor but want to allow object creation with all other overloaded constructors. Then, you can make the empty constructor private and rest of the constructors' public as shown below in the code example.

The object with a parameterized constructor is ok but with empty constructor flashes an error as shown below in the code.

Check out the *Person* class and the *Sample* class given below.

```java
class Person {
    private String name;

    private Person() {

        this.name = "Peter";
    }

    public Person(String name) {
        this.name = name;
    }
}


public class Sample {

    public static void main(String[] args) {

        // Empty constructor is private, so error
        Person peter = new Person(); // Error

        // Parameterized constructor is public, so OK
        Person john = new Person("John");// OK,

    }
}
```

Private Constructor Uses Scenarios

I)Singleton Class Implementation

You know that any class can be made a singleton class that returns a unique object (the same object on different calls). We follow the simple technique to create a singleton class, that is, make the constructors private to stop object creation from outside and provide a **public and static method** that creates and returns the single object of the class. If you wish you can read the Singleton class under quick notes.

II)To stop a class to be inherited (During inheritance, restrict the children, from invoking the private constructor(s)).

If we don't want a class to be inherited, then we can make the class constructor private. So, if we try to derive another class from this class then the compiler will flash an error.

Wondering why the compiler will flash an error?

We know that the order of execution of constructor in inheritance relationship is from the parent to child. When we create an object of a derived class, then the constructor of the base call will be called first and then the constructor of the derived class. Since the base class constructor is private, the derived class object will fail to access the base class constructor.

In the following code example, compiler flashes an error on object creation of the derived class or as soon as you write constructor of the derived class.

```
//base
class B
{
private B()
{
}
}
//Derived
class D extends B
{
public D()
{
}
}
public class Sample {

    public static void main(String[] args) {

        D obj = new D();//error
    }
}
```

NOTE

The preferable way to stop a class to be inherited is to make the class final (the final keyword is in java and the corresponding keyword in C# is sealed). However, the private constructor can also be used in some of the scenarios if occurred in the software application. So, it is good to know about the private constructors.

Q-3) Why are method overloading and method overriding called compile-time and run-time polymorphism respectively? What can be the code example scenarios to illustrate the compile-time and run-time activities?

Answer:

The method overloading and method overriding get resolved at compile time and run time, respectively. That's why we call compile time and run time polymorphism. But, merely stating the definition does not give a clear picture.

Let's see the overloading and overriding code examples that illustrate the compile-time and run-time activities.

Method overloading – Compile time polymorphism:

The code snippet below shows the concept of method overloading where the *Color* method is overloaded.

```
class Paint {
    public void Color() {
    }
    public void Color(int x) {
    }
}
```

In the given example, compiler can easily decide which version of the overloaded method *Color()* or *Color(int x)* should be called at compile time itself.

Let's see by making a call for both methods in the following example.

```java
public class Sample {
    public static void main(String[] args) {
        Paint p = new Paint();
        p.Color(); // line 1
        p.Color(1);// line 2
    }
}
```

By looking at the code in the *main()* method (at line 1 and line 2) and the Paint class, can you tell which version of the *Color* method will be called?

Yes, you can say that line 1 will call *Color* method with empty parameter and line 2 will call *Color* method with one parameter.

Did you run the code? No, without running and looking at the code you've chosen to call the correct version. Similarly, the compiler can decide which version to call at the compile-time without running the program.

Method overriding – Run time polymorphism:

The code snippet given below shows the concept of method overriding. The *run ()* method of the *Car* class is overridden by two subclasses, the *Maruti* and the *Hyundai*. The *drive (Car c)* method of the *Driving* class is receiving multiple types of car objects, such as *Maruti* and *Hyundai*, derived from the *Car* class.

```java
class Driving {

    public void drive(Car c) {
        c.run();
    }
}
class Car {
    public void run() {
        System.out.println("running...");
    }
}
```

```
class Maruti extends Car {
      public void run() {
            System.out.println("Maruti running...");
      }
}
class Hyundai extends Car {
      public void run() {
            System.out.println("Hyundai running...");
      }
}
```

[In case of method overriding, the compiler cannot decide which object's method to execute at compile time. It can decide only at run time.]

By looking at the classes given above i.e. *Car, Maruti,* and *Hyundai* can you tell which object's "*run*" method will be called in the *drive(Car c)* method given below? **Is it the *Maruti* object or the *Hyundai* object?**

```
class Driving {

      public void drive(Car c) {
            c.run();
      }
}
```

You will say, can't decide. So, in the same way, the compiler also cannot decide at compile time. Only if the program is running, the compiler will get to know, which object is coming in the *drive (Car c)* method.

That's why method overriding comes under run time polymorphism.

Q-4) What are the scenarios where a static method is mandatory?

Answer:

You know, to call an instance method of a class, we must need an object of the class. Whereas a static method can be called using the class name only and an object is not required.

In some of the scenarios as given below, we will not be able to create an object of the class, hence using a static method will be mandatory.

- ✓ The *main ()* method (starting point of a program) must be static e.g. *public static void main (String [] args).*

- ✓ In Singleton class.

Elaboration:

1)The *main(String [] args)* method (starting point of a program) must be static:

The *main* method as shown in the code example, the starting point of a program, **must be static** so that the compiler can call it using the class name without creating an object of the class e.g. the class *Sample*. **This is a mandatory situation to use a static method.** If the *main* method is not static, the compiler will not complain, but it will not be able to find the starting point of the program resulting in no program execution.

```
public class Sample {
        public static void main(String[] args) {

        }
}
```

Reason for the *main* method to be static:

The compiler looks for the *main* method first in a program as a starting point for execution.

Consider, if the *main* method is not static in the class *Sample*, then how the compiler will call the *main* method?

To call the *main* method, the compiler needs to create an object of the class *Sample*, then call the *main* method. But it cannot create the object of the class *Sample*, because it must first enter the *main* method.

This is a deadlock situation. So, as a solution, the *main* method is made static, so, it can be called using the class name only.

2)Static method in a Singleton class:

Creating a singleton class is also a scenario where we must need a static method.

In the design of a singleton class, the object creation is stopped from outside of the class and the class itself creates an object of it and returns it to the callers via a public static method to maintain the single unique. You have read the Singleton class with the example under the quick notes section.

The method that returns the object must be static because a caller cannot create an object of the class and can call the method using the class name only.

Q-5) What can be the issue if you delete a base class method if a subclass overrides it?

Answer:

First, let's understand the scenario with a simple example.

In the below code snippet of the table's left column, the subclass *Son* has inherited the *Father* class and uses the methods *useHome()* and *useCar()*.

But, in the table's right column, the *Son* class overrides and defines the method *useCar()*, and at the same time **deletes this method** from the base class *Father*.

```class Father { public void usehome() { } public void useCar() { } } class Son extends Father { }```	```class Father { public void useHome() { } } class Son extends Father { public void useCar() { } }```

The code snippet in **the table's right column illustrates the question being asked, i.e.** the issue if you override a method and delete it from the base class.

In the context of the given example, the **issue is that** there may be a possibility that other siblings might be using the *useCar()* method of the *Father* class that is no longer available to them.

So, following are the scenarios where the issue can occur on performing this activity:

➢ Suppose multiple classes are using the base class throughout the program. If you delete any functionality of the base class, then all the classes will flash an error who is using that.

➢ Second, if you distribute your classes in a library and update the newer version with this activity (deleting a base class method if a subclass overriding it), the existing customers may suffer as their application fails if they use the method.

So, don't delete the base class functionality, instead, you override and define your own definition.

This is the power of method overriding polymorphism feature, that you can easily extend your program feature without breaking the rest of the code.

As a best practice,

We should not delete the functionality of an existing class that we are extending.

However, this should not be a golden rule, but it should be remembered. If you believe and make it clear that this action will not impact the software and that no client code will break or that the functionality of the base class will not be needed in the future, then you can do so.

Q-6) Why use the interface reference for subclass objects while the subclass reference works as well?

Answer:

Read the code below carefully to understand the question. The *TV* and *Tablet* classes are implementing the *Screen* interface.

The question is that if we can create an object of the subclass *TV* with its reference as *TV t = new TV();*

Then, why to use interface reference (base reference) such as *Screen s = new TV();* both are producing the same result as below output:

```
A TV has an LCD Screen
A TV has an LCD Screen
```

```java
interface Screen {
        void setLCD();
}
class TV implements Screen {
        @Override
        public void setLCD() {
                System.out.println("A TV has an LCD Screen");
        }
}

class Tablet implements Screen{

        @Override
        public void setLCD() {
                System.out.println("A    Tablet    has    an    LCD
Screen");
        }
}
```

The *Sample* class shows objects with subclass reference and the base (interface) reference variables.

```
public class Sample {

    public static void main(String[] args) {

        //Subclass object with subclass reference
        TV t = new TV();
        t.setLCD();

        //Subclass object with base (interface)
reference
        Screen s = new TV();
        s.setLCD();
    }
}
```

In fact, we use the base reference when polymorphic implementation is required.

Polymorphic implementation means that you want to decide what subclass object method should be executed at run time.

For example, in a store, you want to show the screen of the TV and Tablet depending upon the objects.

You can write a store class and a show method with the *Screen* interface reference variable as given below.

At the run time, the *show* method will be executed and display the screen depending upon the objects receives for the *TV* and *Tablet* classes.

```
class Store{

    public void show(Screen s){
        s.setLCD();
    }
}
```

Here is the sample that sends TV and Tablet objects to the *show (Screen s)* method of the *Store* class that produces the following output.

```
A TV has an LCD Screen
A Tablet has an LCD Screen
public class Sample {

    public static void main(String[] args) {

        Store s = new Store();
        s.show(new TV());
        s.show(new Tablet());
    }
}
```

As a side note, **the same way** as we used interface reference for its subclasses for polymorphic implementation, the **normal base class reference** and **an abstract class reference** can also be used.

An example using a normal class:

```
class Driver {

    public void drive(Car c) {
        c.run();
    }
}
```

```
class Car {
      public void run() {
            System.out.println("running…");
      }
}

class Maruti extends Car {

      public void run() {
            System.out.println("Maruti running...");
      }

}

class Hyundai extends Car {

      public void run() {
            System.out.println("Hyundai running...");
      }

}
```

NOTE:

If you say that the *show* method can receive the object of the *TV* class as given below and no need to use the interface reference. Yes, you can do so, but what if you want to show the Tablet object? You need to modify the *show* method. Would you like to do modification repeatedly for different classes? This is not a polymorphic implementation.

```
class Store{

      public void show(TV s){
            s.setLCD();
      }
}
```

Q-7) How do polymorphism and inheritance provide extensibility?

Answer:

The new features or behaviours of an application can be easily extended using polymorphism and inheritance concepts. Let's understand the extensibility with an example using each concept separately.

Extensibility using polymorphism.

The features can be easily extended using method overriding polymorphism features.

Consider the below example, the *Sony* and the *Panasonic* classes are using the features *melody song* and *play* of the *Music* class by inheriting it.

```
class Music {

    public void getMelodySong() {
    }
    public void play() {
    }
}


class Sony extends Music {

    public Sony() {
    }
}


class Panasonic extends Music {

    public Panasonic() {
    }
}
```

Now, the requirement for the *Sony* class changes. It no longer wants to use the *play* feature of the *Music* class and wants to define its own *play* feature.

The *play* feature can be easily extended using method overriding concept as below. The *Sony* class overrides and defines its own *play* method.

```
class Sony extends Music {

    public Sony() {
        System.out.println("Sony");
    }

    public void play() {
        System.out.println(" Sony Playing... ");
    }
}
```

Now, the *Sony* class object will call its own *play* method, and not from the *Music* class.

Next, let's have a look at the extensibility using the inheritance properties.

Extensibility using inheritance:

Feature of a program application can be easily extended without touching the well-tested existing classes, saving time and efforts.

To understand how inheritance, give flexibility in extending a feature, read the given program example carefully.

The *Board* class's *write (Marker c)* method accepts the markers object in the *Marker* interface referent variable, to write on it. The program in the *main ()* method, is creating a *BlueMarker* object and sending it to the *write* method of the *Board* class.

```java
class Board {
      public void write(Marker c) {
            c.color();
      }
}

interface Marker {

      void color();
}

class BlueMarker implements Marker {

      public void color() {
            System.out.println("blue");

      }
}

public class Sample {
      public static void main(String[] args) {

            Marker bm = new BlueMarker();
            Board board = new Board();
            board.write(bm);
      }
}
```

As per the current program design, only the blue color marker is supported. Now, you want to extend the feature of the program. You want the support of red marker or green marker etc also.

You can easily extend the support by creating a new class *RedMarker* and implement the *Marker* interface and use it in the program as given below.

New class RedMarker:

```java
class RedMarker implements Marker {

    public void color() {
        System.out.println("red");
    }
}
```

Sample:

```java
public class Sample {

    public static void main(String[] args) {
        Marker bm = new BlueMarker();
        Board board = new Board();
        board.write(bm);

        Marker rm = new RedMarker();
        board.write(rm);

    }
}
```

It should be noted that you did not touch the well-tested existing *Board* class, interface *Marker* or *BlueMarker* class.

So, the extension of the feature is faster with less effort. You can understand it by considering a larger program.

Q-8) Why should anyone use constructor overloading? How does this help?

Answer:

Constructor overloading in object-oriented programming is a powerful concept that enables us to set a default state of the objects differently.

Setting a **default state of an object means**, an object can set the initial value (default value) of the class fields using a constructor.

We'll discuss the following two important reasons for which the constructor overloading is used:

➤ To set a default state of objects.

➤ To maintain backward compatibility of a program.

I) Setting a default state of objects.

Before reading the answer, it is recommended to read the constructor overloading under the quick notes section.

You can set a default state of multiple objects differently using the constructor overloading.

For example, the *Movie* class given below gives the flexibility to set two types of default state for objects, because the class has two overloaded constructors.

```
class Movie {
    private String license;
    public Movie() {
        this.license = null;
    }
    public Movie(String license) {
        this.license = license;
    }
}
```

One default state you can set using the empty constructor. Notice that the *license* field is initialized with default value **null** inside the empty constructor. When you create an object such as *Movie m = new Movie();* the empty constructor will be called implicitly and the null default value will be set to the *license* field.

Another default state can be set using the parameterized constructor. You can set a default value to the *license* field **explicitly** using the one-parameter constructor. When you create an object such as *Movie lm = new Movie("MovieLicense");* the parameterized constructor will be called.

So, we can say that the two types of the default state of objects can be set as below using the overloaded constructors in the *Movie* class.

```
Movie m = new Movie();
Movie lm = new Movie("MovieLicense");
```

You can read the below real-time application example based on the above *Movie* class for more clarity.

Example:

Consider, we have a *Movie* class that plays free movies and premium movies for the users to play. It plays a premium movie based on a valid license.

For the users who want to enjoy the movie for free, you can create an object like *Movie m = new Movie();* for them. Because, the license is not required, and its default value will be set to *null*.

For the premium users, create the object with a valid license and play the movie. Read this code sample.

Code Sample:

```java
public class User {

    public static void main(String[] args) {

        Movie m = new Movie();
        m.playMovie();

        Movie lm = new Movie("MovieLicense");
        lm.playMovie();
    }
}
class Movie {
    private String license;

    public Movie() {
        this.license = null;
    }

    public Movie(String license) {
        this.license = license;
    }

    public void playMovie() {

        if (this.license == "MovieLicense") {

            PlayPremiumMovie();
        } else {
            PlayFreeMovie();
        }
    }
```

```
    private void PlayPremiumMovie() {
        System.out.println("Playing Preminum Movie");
    }

    private void PlayFreeMovie() {

        System.out.println("Playing Free Movie");
    }
}
```

II) Maintaining backward compatibility:

It is helpful in maintaining the backward compatibility of a program. Let's say you have used a constructor to initialize an object of mobile with a brand name as given below, and you have created objects using the statement *Mobile m = **new** Mobile("brand name");* at various places in your program.

```
class Mobile {
    private String brand;

    public Mobile(String brand) {
        this.brand = brand;
    }
    //Methods
    public String getBrand() {
        return brand;
    }
}
```

You later decided to initialize the objects with a brand name and color as well in the new version of the program. For example, *Mobile m = **new** Mobile ("brand name", "color");* then you need to modify the one parameter *Mobile (String brand)* constructor as *Mobile (String brand, String color),* **if you don't overload constructors.**

If you modify the existing constructor, then your code breaks and you need to make changes to the object creation code at all places in the program.

As a solution, you must overload the constructors as shown below.

```
class Mobile {
        private String brand;
        private String color;

        public Mobile(String brand) {
            this.brand = brand;
        }

        public Mobile(String brand, String color) {
            this.brand = brand;
            this.colour = colour;
        }
}
```

Q-9) How does inheritance help eliminate duplicate code?

Answer:

Using the Generalization concept, inheritance can be used to extract duplicate code. This means extracting common properties and functionalities from various classes and placing them in another class that will act as a base class (known as a generalized class).

All the classes will inherit the base class to use those common functionalities.

Let's understand by example.

In the example below, both the *Author* and *Teacher* classes have properties *name* and *age,* and the method *sleep()* that is duplicate.

```java
class Author {
    String name;
    int age;

    public void sleep() {
    }

    public void write() {
    }
}

class Teacher {
    String name;
    int age;

    public void sleep() {
    }

    public void teach() {
    }
}
```

We can move the common fields, *name, age,* and the *sleep ()* methods from the *Author* and *Teacher class* to a new class called *Person*. Both the classes will inherit them from the base class *Person*.

```
class Person {
      protected String name;
      protected int age;

      public void sleep() {
      }
}

class Author extends Person {
      public void write() {
      }
}

class Teacher extends Person {
      public void teach() {
      }
}
```

The common properties and functionalities of the *Author* and *Teacher* classes have been moved to a new class *Person* to avoid duplicate code.

Q-10) Why do you need to overload the method if methods with different names do the task as well?

Answer:

This is true that without method overloading, the task can also be done having different names of the methods. But the method overloading concept is a very powerful feature that provides **code simplicity and readability**.

First, let's consider a code snippet for method overloading and then discuss how it provides code simplicity and readability.

Method overloading code example:

Methods are typically overloaded within a class for variants of the same behaviour. For instance, the behaviour of all the *display* methods of the *Screen* class is the same, i.e. display data, but with different inputs.

```
class Screen {

    public void display(String text) {
        // Display only text
    }

    public void display(Image img) {
        // Display only image
    }

    public void display(String text, Image img) {
        // Display text with image
    }
}
```

```
class Image{

}
```

Simplicity and readability:

We could also have written the distinct names of the methods in the above-mentioned *Screen* class as shown in the examples, Code-1 and Code-2. That will do the same work as well.

Code-1:

```
class Screen {

      public void displayOnlyText(String text) {
      }

      public void displayOnlyImage(Image img) {
      }

      public void displayTextWithImg(String text, Image
img) {
      }
}
```

Code-2:

```
class Screen {

      public void display(String text) {
      }

      public void exhibit(Image img) {
      }

      public void show(String text, Image img) {
      }
}
```

You compare the overloaded *display* methods name of the *Screen* class with the distinct methods name given in the Code-1 and Code-2 examples and decide, which one is simple and readable.

You need to remember all the names of the distinct methods. But you only need to remember one, if you have overloaded the methods.

Secondly, suppose you are used to using the *display* overloaded methods of the *Screen* class in your project. **After months,** your manager asked to display the **text with an image in 3d format** on the screen.

You will create an object, put a dot operator in your editor and have a look at the *display* methods with parameters **as shown below in the snapshot.** Maximum chances are that you are going to respond that 3d format is not supported.

But notice the snapshot again, the format support is already there as the method *public void show (String text, Image img, String format).*

While you were busy with other kinds of stuff, someone else in your team had already implemented it. But he did not overload the *display* method, instead, he used a different name i.e. *show.*

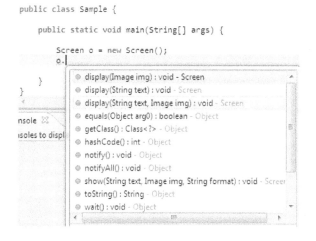

So, as a conclusion,

Using the method overloading is better rather than having a distinct name for the same behaviour, that provides simple and readable code.

Q-11) What are the multiple ways to reuse the code in OOP?

Answer:

The code can be re-used through **class distribution, inheritance** and **composition** concepts. We're going to have a look at each point with examples.

Reusability through class distribution:

You implement a fully functional and tested class once and distribute it in the form of source code and library etc. to others to re-use it. The class can be re-used repeatedly for application development.

For example,

You have written a well-tested and functional player class as given below. You can distribute it to others so they can integrate the class and use it in their applications.

```
class Player{
    public void play(){     }
    public void pause(){ }
    public void stop(){     }
    public void codec(){ }
}
```

Reusability through Inheritance:

Code reuse is also done by the inheritance concept. You can re-use the functionalities of an existing class in your newly create a class by inheriting that.

For example.

You might want to write a brand new *MediaPlayer* class. You can inherit the existing *Player* class and use its functionalities, so, you don't need to rewrite the play, pause, stop, and codec methods, saving time and effort. Just you need to focus on new features of *MediaPlayer*.

```
class MediaPlayer extends Player{

    public void files(){
    }
}
```

Reusability through Composition & Aggregation:

Composition and Aggregation concepts are also used to re-use existing code. For example, the existing classes *Window* and *Door* can be re-used by composing them in a *Room* class.

```
class Room {
    // Room is Composed of objects window and door
    Window window;
    Door door;
}
```

NOTE

You'll read more about the composition and aggregation in the answers to questions #20 & #25.

Q-12) If we can't create an object of an abstract class, then what is its purpose? What can be the scenarios of uses?

Answer:

Yes, it is true that we cannot create an object of an abstract class, but it is a very powerful feature and is designed to **act as a base class**, so, the subclasses can either **use** its defined methods or can **override** them and **implement** the abstract methods if any in the abstract class.

In fact, the **main purpose of an abstract class** is to have common methods defined and enforce subclasses to implement some of its methods (abstract) in software applications.

```
abstract class Beverages {

    public void addMilk() {
        System.out.println("Hot Milk");
    }

    abstract void addIngredient();
}
```

The common methods will be shared by all subclasses. The subclasses can use it or override it for their own definition in case required. The abstract class may have abstract methods to enforce subclasses to implement them.

In the code example given below, the *Tea* and *Coffee* subclasses are using the defined common method *addMilk()* and they are enforced to override and implement the abstract method *void addIngredient()* as well of the abstract class Beverages.

```java
class Tea extends Beverages {

    @Override
    void addIngredient() {
        System.out.println("add Tea");
    }
}
class Coffee extends Beverages {

    void addIngredient() {
        System.out.println("add Coffee");
    }

}
```

Sample Program to use the abstract class

This is the client program that uses the abstract class *Beverages* and the subclasses *Tea* and *Coffee*.

```java
public class Sample {

    public static void main(String[] args) {
        // prepare tea
        System.out.println("---Tea---");
        Beverages t = new Tea();
        t.addMilk();
        t.addIngredient();

        // prepare coffee
        System.out.println("---Coffee---");
        Beverages c = new Coffee();
        c.addMilk();
        c.addIngredient();
    }

}
```

Output:
```
---Tea---
Hot Milk
add Tea
---Coffee---
Hot Milk
add Coffee
```

More Scenarios to use an abstract class:

The previous example was one of the many scenarios of using the abstract class. More **scenarios are given below.**

I. The abstract class can be used to provide a template to subclasses.

II. Secondly, it can also be used to achieve abstraction.

I) Creating a template using an abstract class:

Using an abstract class, you can create a code template that can be used by all the related subclasses.

For example, if you want to provide all the subclasses, an **ordered set of functionalities** to execute, then, you can create a template method in the abstract class that handles the execution order of functionalities.

The template method can contain the execution order of defined methods and abstract methods both.

The below *Document* abstract class contains a template method, *build ().*

```
abstract class Document {
    abstract void setHeader();
    abstract void setBody();
    abstract void setFooter();
```

```
        // Template method
        final public void build() {
                setHeader();
                setBody();
                setFooter();
                format();
        }
        private void format() {
                System.out.println("Format...");
        }
}
```

The *build ()* template method has defined the order of execution of *header*, *body* and *footer* functionalities in addition to the private *format* functionality.

The *Document* abstract class have given responsibility to subclasses to implement the *header*, *body* and *footer* abstract methods.

It should be noted that the *build()* method has been made final, so, no subclasses can override and implement their own version of the *build()* method.

The *Pdf* and *Rtf* subclass will use the *Document* abstract class as given below.

```
class Pdf extends Document {

        @Override
        void setHeader() {
                System.out.println("pdf header");
        }

        @Override
        void setBody() {
                System.out.println("pdf body");
        }
```

```
        @Override
        void setFooter() {
                System.out.println("pdf footer");
        }


}

class Rtf extends Document {

        @Override
        void setHeader() {
                System.out.println("rtf header");
        }

        @Override
        void setBody() {
                System.out.println("rtf body");
        }

        @Override
        void setFooter() {
                System.out.println("rtf footer");
        }
}
```

Following is the sample to test the abstract class with the *build()* template method.

```
public class Sample {
        public static void main(String[] args) {

                Pdf p = new Pdf();
                p.build();

                Rtf r = new Rtf();
                r.build();


        }
}
```

Output
```
pdf header
pdf body
pdf footer
Format...
rtf header
rtf body
rtf footer
Format...
```

NOTE

Using the *Document* abstract class, you cannot create the expected execution order i.e. *header, body, footer*, and *format* in your subclass, because the *format()* method is private.

However, considering the *format ()* method is **public**, are you wondering if you can construct an execution order in subclasses and not use the *build ()* template method of the *Document* abstract class?

Yes, you can construct an execution order of the methods of your choice in the subclass. For example,

```
class Pdf extends Document {

    public void executionOrder() {
        setHeader();
        format();
        setBody();
        format();
        setFooter();
        format();
    }

    @Override
```

```java
    void setHeader() {
        System.out.println("pdf header");
    }

    @Override
    void setBody() {
        System.out.println("pdf body");
    }

    @Override
    void setFooter() {
        System.out.println("pdf footer");
    }
}
```

It's simply a template, designed in the abstract class, and it's up to you if you want to use or not.

II) Achieving abstraction using an abstract class:

In the answer to Question #19, it has been explained how to achieve abstraction using an interface and abstract class.

NOTE

There is a difference between an abstract class and the normal class. Using an abstract class, we can force the core functionalities to the subclasses to implement them. So, whenever a new subclass is created from an abstract class, the compiler will remind us by throwing an error to implement all the essential functionalities if you miss any functionality to implement it. Normal class does not force this constraint.

Additional note

An abstract class can be misused resulting in wastage of time and effort.

I'd like to discuss one scenario I faced in one of the project reviews a long time ago where an abstract class was being misused. During a discussion with the team, I came to know the impact of the misused abstract class.

There was an abstract class called Manager and its seven subclasses such as Music Manager, Video Manager, etc in their own source files in the project.

Initially, someone misused the abstract class and copied a functionality (a defined method in the abstract class) to all the subclasses. Don't know why the programmer did that copy & paste of the same code. Surely, he made a mistake somehow, because a defined method in an abstract class will be shared by all the subclasses and don't need to override the method for the same code. We don't override the defined methods in subclasses unless a subclass needs its own definition for that functionality.

The mistake sounds simple and ignorable as the project still works great.

Let's check out what was the impact due to this mistake.

One day, the client asked the remote team to modify the method as per his changed requirement in the Music module. The team took 2 days' time to modify the method in the Music manager class including testing.

After some time, the client complains that the changed effect he can see in the music module but not in the video module. Again, the team, did the same in the video manager class taking 2 days.

Again, after a week, the same happened for the Playlist module too. then the team realized that the change is required in all the subclasses of the Manager class and they modify all the same in all the subclasses.

It took three weeks to complete the task in practice. It could have been done in the first two days if the duplicate code was not made across all the subclasses of the abstract class.

If all the subclasses were not having their own version of the specific method have the same code and doing the same thing, then only the modification was enough in the abstract class itself.

So, when we are working with an abstract class, we need to have very little focus at least on proper use that can save time and effort.

Q-13) How does encapsulation provide security?

Answer:

Consider an example of a bank account. The *Account* class has a **public** member variable *"balance"*.

```
class Account {
      public double balance;

      public void withdraw () {


      }
}
```

Since the *balance* class field is public, any user class can access it and modify its value. For example, the *User* class has modified the value of the *balance* field as shown below.

```
public class User {
      public static void main(String[] args) {

            Account a = new Account();
            // user can modify the balance of the account,
            // It's a security hole
            a.balance = 2000;
      }
}
```

This is not expected, and **it is a security hole**. Would you like anyone to modify your bank account balance? Of course, not except bank authorities.

So, how can we protect the account balance being modified?

To protect the balance field from illegal direct access, we can encapsulate the *balance* field within a public method.

To encapsulate, we can make the *balance* variable private and can provide its access through a public method e.g. *getBalance()*. Now, no user class will be able to access and change the value of the *balance* variable. He can only read the value of the account balance.

```
class Account {

        private double balance;

        public double getBalance() {

                return balance;
        }

        public void withdraw() {

        }
}
```

As a side note,

You can add more levels of security depending upon requirements. For example, if you want that only authorized bank employees can view the account balance, then in *getBalance()* method, you can write a conditional statement as below.

```
public double getBalance() {

        if( bankEmployee){

                return balance;
        }
        else{
                return 0.0;
        }
}
```

Q-14) Are both the concepts of encapsulation and abstraction really related to hiding complexities? Can you Justify your answer?

Answer:

This is true that they seem to be related to hiding complexities, but, in fact, both are different concepts.

Here are the **correct** definitions for both.

Encapsulation says to hide complexities and internal implementation details from a client(user).

Abstraction says to expose only essential details to the users.

If we consider the abstraction definition as "Expose only essential details to the users and hide the rest(complexities)", then confusion raises and it **seems that** the abstraction is also related to the hiding complexities.

If we write the given statement "Expose only essential details to the users and hide the rest(complexities)" as below, then confusion will be removed.

Expose only essential details to the users and *use encapsulation to hide the complexities.*

So as a conclusion, encapsulation means hiding complexities from the user and abstraction means expose only essential details to the user. That's it.

Let's elaborate more with an example for a clearer picture.

Encapsulation is a technique to hide complexities and internal details. It is an implementation level concept. Abstraction is a design level concept where we decide, what necessary details need to be provided to the users.

Consider the below code example similar to the previous question's example, in which, users such as bank manager and finance department., need to **only** read the customer's account balance.

```
class Account {

    public double balance;

}


public class User {

    public static void main(String[] args) {

        Account user = new Account();
        user.balance = 500;
    }
}
```

For the above classes, let's discuss and make a good design using abstraction and encapsulation concepts.

Since the balance field is **public** in the *Account* class, any user class can modify its value accidentally or intentionally as shown in the example (the user class is modifying the amount of the balance).

This is not expected, and **it is a security hole**. We would not like anyone to modify our bank account balance. Of course not except bank authorities.

So, what is essential to the User class?

The *User* class only wants to read the balance. So, we can only expose a public method e.g. *getBalance()* to them. It will do their job.

So, in this case, the abstraction says that provide them only a *getBalance()* method.

How can we achieve this?

We can achieve this using Encapsulation – by hiding internal details/complexities. We can encapsulate the balance variable inside a public method *getBalance()* and make the *balance* variable private to restrict access.

Better encapsulated code as below.

```
class Account {
      private double balance;

      public double getBalance() {

            return balance;
      }
}

public class User {

      public static void main(String[] args) {

            Account user = new Account();
            user.getBalance();

      }
}
```

As a side note,

notice that in the example above, when we apply encapsulation concept i.e. hiding the internals, we are automatically achieving abstraction.

So, one more point we can make as below.

Encapsulation implements abstraction.

Conclusion:

Hiding complexities are related to the encapsulation. The Abstraction concept says to provide essential details only to users.

Q-15) How should we update a new version of an interface, so the existing client's code does not break?

Answer:

Consider, the **original version** of the Switch interface given below, is distributed to many clients.

```
interface Switch {
     void on();
     void off();
}
```

Now, we want to update the *Switch* interface with a newer version that contains a LED light setting specification too i.e. *"void setLed();"*

How would you upgrade the newer specification *setLed ()?*

Before looking at the good solution, let's see the bad solution first that comes in mind immediately, which is introducing the new method *setLed()* declaration in the *Switch* interface itself.

```
interface Switch{
     void on();
     void off();
     void setLed();
}
```

The problem with this solution is that, if we introduce the new *setLed ()* method specification as given above, the old client's code must break, as you know that **client code must implement all the methods of an interface.**

They will get an error for the unimplemented *setLed()* method at every place, where they have used the *Switch* interface in their applications.

It should be noted that the newer version of an interface should not break the old client code.

So, as the best solution,

we can introduce a new switch, let's say advanced switch, that extends the older *Switch* interface as given below.

```
interface Switch{
     void on();
     void off();
}

interface AdvancedSwitch extends Switch{
     void setLed();
}
```

The *AdvancedSwitch* interface containing *setLed()* method declaration extends the *Switch* interface.

It should be noted that any client implementing the AdvancedSwitch interface must implement all the three methods, i.e. on, off and setLed, because the advanced switch has extended the Switch interface.

Old clients will be happy:

The new version of the library will not break the old client's application. Old clients were using the *Switch* interface as below. If they use the newer version, it will not affect their code.

```
class oldClient implements Switch{

     @Override
     public void on() {
     }

     @Override
     public void off() {
     }
}
```

NOTE

I) If some of the old clients want to use the newer version, they can implement both the interfaces i.e. *Switch* and *AdvancedSwitch* as shown in the code below. Just they have to implement *setLed()* method and recompile the code.

```
class oldClient implements Switch, AdvancedSwitch{

    @Override
    public void on() {
    }

    @Override
    public void off() {
    }

    @Override
    public void setLed() {
    }
}
```

Or they can also modify the existing declaration and use as "**class** *oldClient* **implement** *AdvancedSwitch*" instead of "**class** *oldClient* **implements** *Switch, AdvancedSwitch*".

The new clients can implement only the *AdvanceSwitch* interface as below.

```java
class NewClient implements AdvancedSwitch{

    @Override
    public void setLed () {
    }

    @Override
    public void on() {
    }

    @Override
    public void off() {

    }
}
```

II) As shown below, we could have provided a distinct interface as another working solution. It won't break old client code either. But, as provided in the best solution at the beginning, it is a good idea to have **associated specifications together.**

```java
interface Switch{
    void on();
    void off();
}


interface AdvancedSwitch{
    void setLed();
}
```

Q-16) Which one is a good choice if you have an option to choose between an interface and an abstract class and why?

Answer:

Let's see an example where both an interface and an abstract class can be an option to choose.

Below are a *Charger* interface and a *Charger* abstract class, each with a *charge* () method. It is pre-decided that the abstract class will not have any defined method, and both will have contracts only.

```
interface Charger {
    void charge();
}
```

```
abstract class Charger {
    abstract void charge();
}
```

If you need to create a *Mobile* class and implement the *charge()* method, then you can choose either of them between the interface and the abstract class.

So, the question is which one is the best choice between the interface and the abstract class and what can be the reasons?

As an answer, the best choice should be the interface due to the following reasons:

Reason-1)

You know that Java and C# like languages do not support multiple inheritance using classes. Meaning, you cannot inherit more than one class. However, you can inherit and implement multiple interfaces.

So, if you choose the abstract class, then we are losing a chance of inheriting another class if required in the future. For example, the *Mobile* class given below has inherited the abstract class *Charger*, hence it lost a chance to inherit another class. For example, if you are required to inherit a class e.g. Gadget, you cannot inherit that.

```
class Mobile extends Charger{
      // extended the abstract class,
      // no more class can be inherited.
}
```

Whereas, in the case of using the interface, we have a chance to inherit a class.

```
class Mobile implements Charger{
      // Implemented interface, have a chance
      //to inherit a class if required.
}
```

If you are required to inherit the *Gadget* class, then you can do so as below.

```
class Gadget {

}
```

```
class Mobile extends Gadget implements Charger {

      @Override
      public void charge() {

      }
}
```

Reason-2)

If we choose the abstract class, the original design may be violated by a programmer.

When a new programmer comes out later, he can alter the abstract class and introduce a new method with a definition. But, as per the original design, mentioned in the example at the beginning, the intention of the abstract class was to have only a contract and no defined method.

If he does the same with the interface, he will be warned by the compiler or he already knows he can't define a method in the interface.

"If you have an option to choose between an interface and an abstract class, always prefer the interface."

Q-17) What are the main aims of using an interface? Do we really use interface variables? If so, for what?

Answer:

Following are the main aims of using an interface:

- ✓ To enforce a class to implement the specific functionalities
- ✓ To add a level of abstraction.

Enforcing classes to implement essential functionality:

If you want to enforce classes to implement specific functionalities, then we need to use an interface.

(*Note that abstract class is also used to enforce some functionalities, but it is different than an interface – I believe you should not have doubt after reading the answers to questions #12 and #16*).

For example, if we want to develop different types of a mouse such as an optical mouse, wireless mouse, trackball mouse and want **to make sure that** each mouse has *left-click, right-click* and *scroll* functionality, then an interface helps here.

```
interface Mouse {
        void leftClick();
        void rightClick();
        void scroll();
}
```

Each mouse class will, therefore, implement the interface and define **all** its methods. If even a single method implementation of the interface is **missed** by any mouse class, the compiler will alert with an error. This is how an interface ensures that the essential functionalities have been implemented by each class.

Again, **an interface ensures** that a programmer does not forget to implement all essential functionalities while developing a class and implementing it.

Assume, an interface has 10 declarations of methods. If, while implementing it, the interface **does not force** the programmer to define all the methods in his class, then there is a possibility that he will miss defining some of the methods.

Code Example:

```java
interface Mouse {
    void leftClick();
    void rightClick();
    void scroll();
}


class Optical implements Mouse {

    @Override
    public void leftClick() {
        System.out.println("Left Click");
    }

    @Override
    public void rightClick() {
        System.out.println("Right Click");
    }

    @Override
    public void scroll() {
        System.out.println("Scroll");
    }
```

```
        private void handleLED() {
                // internal method
        }
}

public class Sample {
        public static void main(String[] args) {
                Optical om = new Optical();
                om.leftClick();
                om.rightClick();
                om.scroll();
        }
}
Output:
Left Click
Right Click
Scroll
```

Adding a level of abstraction:

Separating a client code from implementation is one of the main aims of an interface. It abstracts the class implementation from the client code.

For example, the *Screen* class given below is a client who is using the concrete class *ArrayList* (class implementation) to display its elements.

```
class Screen {
        public static void display (ArrayList list) {

        }
}
```

Note that the client knows directly about the *ArrayList*. Problem is that the client cannot use another kind of list such as linked list until we modify the client code. Isn't it a bad idea to modify the client code over and over when a different list is required?

So, we can separate the implementation from the client code using an interface. Also, you can say that we can abstract the implemented classes using an interface. You know that the List interface is implemented by the *ArrayList* and *LinkedList* both. Hence, we can use the *List* interface as below.

```
class Screen {
    public static void display (List list) {
    }
}
```

Now, the implementations are abstracted from the client code. The client only knows what a list does but does not know how they have been implemented. You can pass different types of list and you don't require to modify the client code repeatedly.

Why did I say adding a level of abstraction?

Because a class (e.g. *ArrayList*) itself has abstracted its data and methods implementation by encapsulating them. We are adding more levels of abstraction using an interface by hiding the concrete classes such as *ArrayList* and *LinkedList*.

Do we use interface variables?

Yes, we do use interface variables in an application. Typically, we keep collections of related constants in an interface. We use these variables using the interface name with dot operator e.g. *Math.PI* in the program.

In fact, personally, I have used tons of interfaces, grouped with related constant variables in a large software library product.

```
interface Math{
    public static final double      PI = 3.14;
    public static final double ELUERNUMBER = 2.718;
    public static final double SQRT = 1.41421;
}
```

NOTE

By default, the variables in an interface are public, static, and final that you don't need to write. However, as a best practice, we write them just for readability purposes in a program.

Q-18) What are impacts if I don't follow dictum – "Code to the interface, not to the implementation"?

Answer:

The meaning of "code to the interface, not to the implementation" is that, if you have an option to choose between an interface and a concrete class, then choose the interface. The implementation intent here is a concrete / specific class.

If we **don't use an interface** instead of implementation, the **impact is that** the code will be tightly coupled **resulting in a problem in extending a new feature or maintaining the existing classes.**

(Tightly coupled means, a class is highly depended on another class. If you make changes to one class, another will be affected. The reverse of it is the loose coupling in which you reduce the dependencies.)

We're going to understand this by example scenarios. So, first of all, let's see some codes that use concrete classes that are tightly coupled and what are the issues because of them and their solutions by coding to the interface.

Code to implementation (Concrete classes):

We'll see two code examples under Code-1 and Code-2 sections that demonstrate code to implementation and the issues because of this.

Code-1:

Given below is a scenario, in which a game should display multiple types of scenes.

In the given code example, the *Game* class has been coded to the implementations. In other words, there are two concrete classes in the *Game* class, a *HouseScene* and a *ParkScene*.

The following are the issues because of coding to concrete classes (implementation). First, read the code example given below carefully before reading the issues.

I) If we remove any of the *HouseScene* or *ParkScene* class, the *Game* class won't function, as it depends on both the classes. – Maintenance issue.

II) If we want to **extend the feature** by introducing a new class e.g. *SuperMarketScene*, then we **must modify the code** of the *Game* class. – Extensibility issue.

```
class Game {

        HouseScene hs;
        ParkScene ps;

        public Game(HouseScene hs, ParkScene ps) {

                this.hs = hs;
                this.ps = ps;
        }

        public void ShowScene() {

                hs.getScene();
                ps.getScene();
        }
}

class HouseScene {

        public void getScene() {
                System.out.println("House Scene…");
        }
}
```

```java
class ParkScene {

    public void getScene() {
        System.out.println("Park Scene…");
    }
}
```

Code-2:

The *Screen* class's *display* method is receiving a concrete class *ArrayList* to print its elements. So, it's a code to implementation.

```java
class Screen {

    public static void display(ArrayList list) {

        System.out.println(list.toString());
    }
}
```

The issue because of the code to implementation is that the *display* method strongly depends upon the *ArrayList* class. If we want to use another list container e.g. *LinkList* class, then we need to modify the *display* method as the *display(LinkedList list)*. This is creating a problem of maintenance. You must modify the *Screen* class.

You understand the maintenance and extensibility issues because of the coding to implementations.

Let's see how coding to interface helps avoid these issues. We'll apply the code to interface principle on the same code examples given in Code-1 and Code-2 above.

In both examples, we'll use an interface (code to interface) instead of the concert class (code to implementations).

Code to interface:

Code-1:

We have created a new interface *Scene* and the classes *HouseScene* and the *ParkScene* have implemented the interface.

In the *ShowScene(Scene s)* method of the *Game* class, the interface *Scene* reference variable is introduced.

```
interface Scene {
    void getScene();
}


class HouseScene implements Scene {

    public void getScene() {
        System.out.println("House Scene...");
    }
}


class ParkScene implements Scene {

    public void getScene() {
        System.out.println("Park Scene...");
    }
}


class Game {

    public void ShowScene(Scene s) {
        s.getScene();
    }
}

//TEST
```

```java
public class Sample {

    public static void main(String[] args) {

        Scene hs = new HouseScene();
        Scene ps = new ParkScene();
        Game g = new Game();
        g.ShowScene(hs);
        g.ShowScene(ps);


    }
}
```

Now, we coded to an interface. The *Game* class does not know the concrete classes *HouseScene* and the *ParkScene* directly as we used the *Scene* interface.

Let's verify how did coding to interface resolve the issues of maintenance and extensibility?

If you remove any scene e.g. *ParkScene*, the *Game* class does not need modification. This resolves maintenance issues.

If you want to extend a new class e.g. *SuuperMarketScene,* just you have to implement the interface *Scene* as shown below. You don't have to change the existing classes *Game, HouseScene,* and the *ParkScene.*

```java
class SuperMarketScene implements Scene {

    public void getScene() {
        System.out.println("Super Market Scene...");
    }
}
```

Code-2:

In the display method of the *Screen* class, you can replace the *ArrayList* class parameter with the *List* interface i.e. from the `display(ArrayList list)` to `display(List list)`.

Now, the *Screen* class supports both types of the list such as *ArrayList* and *LinkedList*. Because, both the classes implement the *List* interface.

Any container class who implements the *List* interface can be used in the program without modification of the *Screen* class.

```
class Screen {

    public static void display(List list) {

        System.out.println(list.toString());
    }
}
```

Following is the sample example that demonstrates the use of the *Screen* class with *ArrayList* and *LinkedList*.

```
//TEST
public class Sample {

    public static void main(String[] args) {

        ArrayList al = new ArrayList();
        al.add("Apple");
        al.add("Mango");
        al.add("Orange");
        System.out.println("ArrayList ");
        Screen.display(al);

        LinkedList ll = new LinkedList();
        ll.add("Apple");
        ll.add("Mango");
        ll.add("Orange");
        System.out.println("LinkedList ");
        Screen.display(ll);

    }
}
```

Output:
ArrayList
[Apple, Mango, Orange]
LinkedList
[Apple, Mango, Orange]

As a good practice, always try to code to the interface, not to the implementation.

NOTE

The original phrase: program to an interface, not an implementation is mentioned in the GoF book in which Erich Gamma is the co-author.

I'd like to provide a following additional note on it.

ADDITIONAL NOTE

You should try to implement an interface if you write a new feature in a project or something writing from scratch.

However, in my opinion, don't try to convert the code implemented to concrete classes to interfaces in an existing project or modules that are already working, or whenever you find the "code to implementation". Because it will take time and effort refactoring and testing the code. If you're working in an organization, just you can notify your executive and leave it up to him to act. If you are working on your project, you are responsible to decide.

Q-19) How can an "interface" or an "abstract class", be used to aid in improving the degree of abstraction in the design of a class?

Answer:

We'll understand how an interface or abstract class can be used to achieve abstraction with a simple code example.

In the answer to the previous question #18, you have already understood how useful an interface is instead of using concrete classes. We'll take a similar example to explain and understand how abstraction can be achieved by using an interface or an abstract class.

For better understanding, we will begin the explanation from a non-abstract code to an abstract code.

Below is a code example for a scenario, in which a board class uses a marker to write on it.

The *Board* class in its *write* method accepts a *BlueMarker* concrete class object.

```
class Board {

    public void write(BlueMarker m) {
        m.color();
    }
}


class BlueMarker {

    public void color() {
        System.out.println("blue..");
    }
}
```

Note that the *BlueMarker* **class is not abstracted from the** *Board* **class**, because the *Board* class knows the *BlueMarker* class directly in the *write* method.

Hence, the *Board* class cannot use markers of different color e.g. Red Marker or Green marker but Blue color only.

If we need to use markers of different colors, then we must modify the write method of the Board class over and over.

This is really a bad design of classes. Isn't it?

By the way, would you like to buy a brand new board every time you want to use markers of a different color? Your answer must be a "big no".

As a good design, we can abstract the concrete implementation of a marker class from the *Board* class using an interface, so, the *Board* class does not need to modify repeatedly to use markers of different colors.

Achieving abstraction:

Simply create a new *Marker* interface. It will be implemented by all specific marker classes as shown below.

```java
interface Marker {

        void color();
}


class BlueMarker implements Marker {

        public void color() {
                System.out.println("blue..");

        }
}
```

In the *Board* class's *write* method replace the *BlueMarker* object reference with the *Marker* interface i.e. *write(BlueMarker m)* with *write(Marker c)* as shown here.

```
class Board {
    public void write(Marker c) {
        c.color();
    }
}
```

Now, **the specific Marker classes are abstracted from the *Board* class**. The *Board* class knows nothing about the concrete classes such as the *BlueMarker*, *GreenMarker*, *RedMarker* and receives their objects in the *Marker* interface reference.

Now, if we need to use a new marker of different color e.g. *RedMarker*, then simply create a class and implement the *Marker* interface as shown below. Note that the *Board* class no longer need modification on introducing a new *RedMarker* class, **because we have achieved abstraction using the *Marker* interface**. All concrete (specific classes) are abstracted from the *Board* class.

Code:

```
class RedMarker implements Marker{
    public void color() {

        System.out.println("red..");
    }
}
```

Following is the sample code that uses different color markers to write on the Board.

```
public class Sample {

    public static void main(String[] args) {

        Marker blueMarker = new BlueMarker();
        Board board = new Board();
        board.write(blueMarker);

        Marker redMarker = new RedMarker();
        board.write(redMarker);
    }
}
```

With an abstract class, abstraction can also be accomplished in the same manner as with an interface as per need.

Q-20) Both the composition and aggregation follow the Has-A relationship, then how are they different? Which one should you choose when?

Answer

We'll understand the two differences between composition and aggregation considering the following points with code examples.

1. Strong and weak bonding(relationship) between objects.

2. Ownership of objects.

You know that there are relationships between classes such as Association, Composition, and Aggregation that form HAS-A relationship. You used to say that X object is associated with Y object etc. Right? Both the composition and aggregation are in fact association relationships.

[*Has-A relationship means, an object is composed of other one or more objects. For example, a room is composed of windows and doors. In other words, a room HAS A window and a room HAS A door, etc. As another example, a car HAS A driver*]

The composition follows a strong Has-A (strong association) relationship whereas the aggregation follows a weak Has-A (weak association) relationship.

Why do we say strong and weak relationships?

Because, in composition, the main object holds the ownership and decides the life cycle of the composed objects. Meaning, if an object is destroyed all its composed objects must also be destroyed. So, there is a strong bonding or relationship between parent and composed child objects.

In Aggregation, all composed objects **have their own life cycle**, that's why it forms a weak relationship.

Let's understand the ownership of a life cycle and relationships of an object for both the composition and aggregation by example.

Composition:

In the below code example, the *Room* class has composed two objects i.e. the *Window* and the *Door* class. If the *Room* object is destroyed, then the *Window* and the *Door* objects must also be destroyed. Meaning, the *Room* object decides the life cycle of the *Window* and the *Door* objects.

```java
class Room {
        // Room is Composed of objects window and door
        Window window;
        Door door;
        public Room() {
                System.out.println("Room is composed of ");
                this.door = new Door();
                this.window = new Window();
        }

        public void DisplayRoom() {
                this.door.setDoor();
                this.window.setWindow();
        }
}

class Door {
        public void setDoor() {
                System.out.println("Door...");
        }
}
```

```java
class Window {
      public void setWindow() {
            System.out.println("Window...");
      }
}


public class Sample {
      public static void main(String[] args) {

            Room room = new Room();
            room.DisplayRoom();
      }
}
```

The output of the above code will be as below:
Room is composed of
Door...
Window...

Note that the objects of the *Window* and the *Door* class have been created inside the *Room* class. Hence, when the room object will be garbage collected, then door and window objects will also be garbage collected.

Make a point that, by declaring the *Window* and the *Door* class variables as below in the *Room* class does not mean that it is composed. It will be **true only if** the *Room* object holds the ownership of them or else it will be said that they are aggregated.

```java
class Room {

      Window window;
      Door door;
}
```

Aggregation:

In the Aggregation, all the composed objects should not be bonded to destroy on main object destruction. All composed Objects have their own life cycle.

For example, a car should have a driver. If the car is destroyed, the composed object, the driver should not be destroyed. So, the car HAS-A driver forms a weak HAS-a relationship.

```java
class Driver {

    public void drive() {
        System.out.println("drive...");
    }
}


class Car {
    Driver d;
    public void setDriver(Driver d) {
        this.d = d;
    }

    public void move() {
        this.d.drive();
    }
}

public class Sample {
    public static void main(String[] args) {

        Car c = new Car();
        Driver d = new Driver();
        c.setDriver(d);
```

```
            c.move();
            // delete Car
            c = null;
            // driver object is still alive
            d.drive();
        }
}
```

The *Car* and *Driver* objects are created in the *main ()* method, and the car has set a driver via the *setDriver(Driver d)* method. The Car variable *c* has been set to *null*, so it can be garbage collected and check if the driver object is alive. You'll find the driver object still exists, so it's got its own life cycle.

We read the example of aggregation with a class driver aggregated in the car class.

The aggregation can also be used with interfaces. Read the below topic.

Aggregation using interfaces:

Aggregation can also be implemented using interfaces. The Car class given below contains two variables of the Driver interface and Fuel interface written in the code example.

In this example also, the Car object does not own the life cycle of the Driver and Fuel interfaces. Hence, utilizing the aggregation concept.

```
class Car {
        // interfaces
        Driver d;
        Fuel f;
        public void setDriver(Driver d) {
                this.d = d;
        }
```

```
    public void setFuel(Fuel f) {
        this.f = f;
    }

    public void fillFuel() {
        this.f.fill();
    }

    public void move() {
        this.d.drive();
    }
}
```

In the *main ()* method as shown below, the *Car, ExperiencedDriver* and *Petrol* class objects have been created. The references of the *ExperiencedDriver* and *Petrol* objects have been passed to the *Car* class methods *setDriver* and *setFuel*.

```
public class Sample {
    public static void main(String[] args) {

        Car c = new Car();
        Driver d = new ExperiencedDriver();
        Fuel f = new Petrol();
        c.setDriver(d);
        c.setFuel(f);

        c.fillFuel();
        c.move();
    }
}
```

Here are interfaces used in the above code example to demonstrate aggregation.

```java
interface Fuel {
    void fill();
}

class Petrol implements Fuel {

    @Override
    public void fill() {

        System.out.println("Filling Petrol");

    }
}

interface Driver {
    void drive();
}

class ExperiencedDriver implements Driver {

    @Override
    public void drive() {
        System.out.println("Experienced Driver drives
the Car");
    }
}
```

Which one would you choose and when?

Now you understand when to use composition and aggregation by reading their concepts and example.

However, **as a conclusion,** during the class design, if you think that a parent object should own the life cycle of the composed child objects, then use composition. If the parent object does not hold the child's life cycle, then use aggregation.

It should be noted that the composition and aggregation both are in fact a design concept in which we consider the HAS-A relationship and ownership of the life cycle of the child objects. By **merely** composing the child objects into a parent class, you cannot say that if the composition or the aggregation concept has been applied. For example,

```
class Room {

        Window window;
        Door door;
}
```

Q-21) In what scenarios inheritance is indispensable? Is it true that inheritance is used for code re-use only? If not, what are the other factors?

Answer:

We'll have a look at some situations where inheritance is indispensable with example and the factors where inheritance is used besides code re-use.

If you need to implement an interface or use an abstract class (designed to use as a base class), then you **must use** inheritance. You don't have other options.

Interface example:

The *PiGraph* class inherits and implements the *draw()* method of the *Graph* interface.

```
interface Graph {
      public void draw();
}


class PiGraph implements Graph{
      public void draw() {
            System.out.println("PI Graph");
      }
}
```

Abstract class example:

The *Tea* and *Coffee* classes inherit the *Beverages*, abstract class.

```
abstract class Beverages {
      public void addMilk() {
            System.out.println("Hot Milk");
      }
```

```
        abstract void addIngredient();
}
class Tea extends Beverages {

        @Override
        void addIngredient() {
                System.out.println("add Tea");
        }
}
class Coffee extends Beverages {

        void addIngredient() {
                System.out.println("add Coffee");
        }
}
```

A class wants to implement Multiple interfaces:

A class can implement multiple interfaces. In the below example, there are two interfaces *Flyable* and *Eatable*. The class Bird inherits and implements the methods of both the interfaces.

Following is the declaration of implementing both interfaces by the *Bird* class: "**class** Bird **implements** Flyable, Eatable"

Code sample:

```
interface Flyable {
        void fly();
}

interface Eatable {
        void eat();
}
```

```java
// CLASS- Bird class will implement both interfaces
class Bird implements Flyable,Eatable {

        public void fly() {
                System.out.println("Bird flying");
        }

        public void eat() {
                System.out.println("Bird eats");
        }
        // It can have more own methods.
}

public class Sample {

        public static void main(String[] args) {

                Bird b = new Bird();
                b.eat();
                b.fly();
        }
}
```

An interface extends interface:

An interface can also inherit another interface by extending it.

For example,

The interface *B* is extending another interface *A*. Note that the interface uses "extends" keyword not "implements" keyword to extend another interface.

Whereas, a class uses the "implements" keyword to implement an interface.

```
interface A {
    void fa();
}

interface B extends A {
    void fb();
}
```

Is it true that inheritance is used for code re-use only?

The first thing that comes into mind when we talk about the concept of inheritance is, the reuse of code i.e. inherit a class and use its all public properties and behaviours.

In fact, inheritance is a fundamental part of object-oriented programming and it's a powerful concept that is used not only for code reusability but also in **eliminating code redundancy, feature extensibility** and **implementation hiding** (abstraction), etc.

Eliminating code redundancy

In the answer to question #9, you have already seen how to remove the redundant code using the concept of generalization that utilizes the inheritance concept. The Author and Teacher class common properties and methods were moved to a new class Person to eliminate the redundant codes.

Feature extensibility

In the answer to question #7, you have read how the inheritance helps in feature extensibility with minimal effort and time using the inheritance concept. The markers of different colors are getting extended easily and used in the Board class without modifying other classes.

Implementation hiding (abstraction)

In the answer to question #19, we have seen that an interface and abstract class are used to achieve abstraction. In fact, to use the interface and abstract class, the inheritance concept is used.

Q-22) Is really multi-level inheritance used? What can be an example of it in real-time?

Answer:

Yes, the multi-level inheritance is used in real-time though the frequency of requirement may be less than that of the single inheritance.

Here is a real-time scenario where the use of multi-level inheritance fits the best.

Scenario:

A book publisher has different price packages for the services i.e. Silver, Gold, and Diamond to publish a book.

Packages and Services:

Silver	Gold	Diamond
IsbnAllocaiton Publish Sale	All services available in Silver Copyright	All services available in Gold Promotion

From the package and service table, you can observe that the Gold package is accessing all the services from the Silver and the Diamond package is accessing all the services from Gold.

Hence, we can use a multi-level inheritance concept. Silver <- Gold <- Diamond.

Following is the design of classes using multiple inheritance.

```
class Silver {
      public void IsbnAllocaiton() {
            System.out.println("ISBN Allocation");
      }

      public void Publish() {
            System.out.println("Publish");
      }

      public void Sale() {
            System.out.println("Sale");
      }
}

class Gold extends Silver {

      void copyright() {
            System.out.println("Copyright");

      }
}

class Diamond extends Gold {
      void Promotion() {
            System.out.println("Promotion");

      }
}
```

If you create an object of the bottom class *Diamond*, the features of all its super classes will be available. The following code demonstrates this.

```
public class BookPublisher {
```

```
public static void main(String[] args) {
        Diamond d = new Diamond();
        d.IsbnAllocaiton();
        d.Promotion();
        d.Sale();
        d.copyright();
        d.Publish();
    }
}
```

Q-23) How should an interface be designed so that no client is compelled to depend on specifications that it does not use?

Answer:

If you're my client. Would you love it if you are forced to use something you don't need? Your reply wouldn't, of course.

For the same reason, while designing an interface, we must bear in mind that no client (class) is compelled to define the methods that they do not use.

You know that an interface forces you to **define all its specifications(methods)** when you create a class and implement the interface. So, when we write an interface, we should think if there is any scenario where a client is compelled to define all the methods of the interface, even though some of the methods are useless to him.

Let's see a scenario, where some clients may not want to use all the methods of the interface but forced to define them.

Consider the design of the following food menu interface. It will be used by restaurants.

```
interface Menu {
    void getVegMenu();
    void getNonVegMenu();
}
```

All the restaurants who use the menu interface must implements it's both methods.

So far it is pretty clear and sounds good.

Now, let's see if there is a glitch in the interface.

There are two restaurants, the *Spicy* and the *Vegy*. The *Spicy* restaurant offers vegetarian and non-vegetarian food, and the *Vegy* restaurant offers only vegetarian food.

Both the *Spicy* and the *Vegy* restaurants implement the interface *Menu*.

But there is an issue with some clients.

For the *Spicy* restaurant, it is ok to override and define both the methods *getVegMenu*() and *getNonVegMenu*() of the interface Menu, as it offers both veg and non-veg food.

But there is an issue with the *Vegy* restaurant. It requires to override and define only *getVegMenu*() method, but, it is forced to override and define the *getNonVegMenu*() method also, **which is unnecessary** for the *Vegy* restaurant.

So, our interface design is not so good.

So, what can we do, so that, the *Vegy* restaurant is not forced to define the *getNonVegMenu* () method?

It's simple.

We can split and segregate the *Menu* interface into two parts. e.g. *VegMenu* and *NonVegMenu* as given below.

```
interface VegMenu {
    void getVegMenu();
}


interface NonVegMenu {
    void getNonVegMenu();
}
```

Now, the *Spicy* class can implement both the interfaces, so, it can override and define both the methods *getVegMenu()* and *getNonVegMenu()*.

```java
class Spicy implements VegMenu, NonVegMenu {

    @Override
    public void getNonVegMenu() {

    }

    @Override
    public void getVegMenu() {

    }
}
```

The *Vegy* class can implement the *VegMenu* interface only, so it can define only *getVegMenu()* method.

```java
class Vegy implements VegMenu {

    @Override
    public void getVegMenu() {

    }
}
```

NOTE

This is an example of one of the oop design principles called **ISP** – Interface Segregation Principle.

It states that no client should be forced to depend on methods it does not use – Wikipedia.

Make fine grained interfaces that are client-specific. - Robert C. martin

Q-24) How can inheritance break the client code, but composition cannot? Illustrate the scenario example of this.

Answer:

If the client code uses the classes that are designed using inheritance, there is a chance that it can break the client code, where classes designed using composition cannot.

We will see an example scenario in which inheritance breaks the client code. Using the same example by composition, we will see the same client code working. **Note that** we'll not change the client code in both the cases i.e. when we use designed classes with inheritance hierarchy and using composition.

Actually, why the client code will break when we use inheritance and not the composition?

You know that the child class depends upon the parent class in an inheritance relationship, and in the composition, the main class depends on the composed classes.

So, if we make changes in the parent class, then the child classes and client code also suffer. Similarly, if you make changes in the composed class, the main class will suffer.

But there is some scenario in which if you make changes in the base class in an **inheritance hierarchy**, the client code will suffer, but it will not be the case when we use composition.

Let's check it out...

Scenario example using inheritance:

Read the below code carefully and then we'll see how making changes in the Job base class affecting the client code.

The *TechnicalJob* class has inherited the *Job* base class. The *Sample* class (client code) has created an object of the *TechnicalJob* child class and invoked the *jobCount()* method of the *Job* class to get the number of jobs available. **Note that** the *jobCount()* method return data type is **int**.

```java
class Job {
        private int count;

        // Return number of jobs
        public int jobCount() {

                this.count = findJobs();
                return this.count;
        }

        private int findJobs() {
                // Pretend found jobs from a database
                return this.count = 100;
        }
}

class TechnicalJobs extends Job {

}

// Client code
public class Sample {

        public static void main(String[] args) {

                TechnicalJobs j = new TechnicalJobs();
                int count = j.jobCount();
                System.out.println("Jobs found =" + count);
        }
}
```

Consider, the design requirement is changed and the decision has been made to move the internal *findJob()* method of the *Job* base class to a brand new separate *Search* class. The designer wants to keep the job searching functionality from the database separate from the *Job* class.

The newly designed *Search* class with the base class *Job* will now look like below.

```java
class Search {
        private int count;

        public int getCount() {

                findJobs();

                return count;
        }

        private void findJobs() {
                this.count = 100;
        }

}

class Job {

        // Return number of jobs
        public Search jobCount() {

                return new Search();
        }
}

class TechnicalJobs extends Job {

}
```

Look at the below *Sample* class the same as earlier. *The jobCount()* method returns the *Search* class datatype now. It was returning the int data type, before newly designed classes.

Hence, the client code breaks.

```
// Client code
public class Sample {

    public static void main(String[] args) {

        TechnicalJobs j = new TechnicalJobs();
        int count = j.jobCount();
        System.out.println("Jobs found =" + count);

    }
}
```

Repeating, if we change the return type of the *jobCount* method of the base class from int to a class type **e.g.** *Search* **class type (e.g. public int** *jobCount()* to *public Search jobCount()* **)**, then the client code will break and throw an error at the statement *int count = j.jobCount();* in the *main()* method.

Now, let's check the same scenario example using the composition.

Scenario example using composition:

Here the *TechnicalJob* class will compose the *Job* class.

```
class Job {
    private int count;

    // Return number of jobs
    public int jobCount() {

        this.count = findJobs();
```

```
                return this.count;
        }

        private int findJobs() {
                // Pretend found jobs from a database
                return this.count = 100;
        }
}

class TechnicalJobs {
        // Composed the Job class
        private Job j = new Job();

        public int jobCount() {

                return j.jobCount();
        }
}

// Client code
public class Sample {

        public static void main(String[] args) {

                TechnicalJobs j = new TechnicalJobs();
                int count = j.jobCount();
                System.out.println("Jobs found =" + count);
        }
}
```

If we introduce the *Search* class now, the *TechnicalJob* class will require little modification, but the client code will not break. Have a look at the changed design. Notice that the below *Sample* class code is exactly the same as the previous *Sample* class code.

Code after the change:

```
class Search {
      private int count;

      public int getCount() {

             findJobs();

             return count;
      }

      public void findJobs() {
             this.count = 100;
      }

}


class Job {

      // Return number of jobs
      public Search jobCount() {

             return new Search();
      }
}

class TechnicalJobs {
      // Composed the Job class
      private Job j = new Job();

      public int jobCount() {
```

```
            // little modification
            return j.jobCount().getCount();
      }
}


// Client code
public class Sample {

      public static void main(String[] args) {

            TechnicalJobs j = new TechnicalJobs();
            int count = j.jobCount();
            System.out.println("Jobs found =" + count);

      }
}
```

This was just a demonstration scenario where I wanted to show that inheritance can fail but not the composition that helps us decide what to choose in that scenario.

Does it mean that you shouldn't use inheritance?

Not at all, it does not mean that you shouldn't use inheritance or always choose composition over inheritance. Both have their own roles. You have already read the scenarios where inheritance is indispensable in the answer to question #21.

Repeating the said statements at the start in another way.

It is true that the subclasses highly depend upon the base class or say tightly coupled with the base class in an inheritance relationship. In fact, this applies to the composition as well, that is the main class depends upon the composed classes.

If you make any changes to the base class, then the subclasses will also get affected. If you make any changes to the composed class, then the main class can also get affected.

For example, suppose the child class Y has inherited the base class X using inheritance, and the main class Y has composed the X class in composition.

If you change a method name in the X class, the Y class will fail in both inheritance and composition. If you change the algorithms of a method in the X class, it will also affect both.

As a conclusion,

In both inheritance and composition, you can find the tightly coupled code but as a scenario, as you have seen in the example, the composition wins for flexibility and maintainability.

I'll recommend reading the answer to questions #20 that details about the composition and question #25 for good guidelines to use inheritance and composition.

Q-25) What are the good guidelines to choose inheritance or composition?

Answer:

The answer includes good guidelines for using inheritance, composition, and aggregation. It will illustrate how to choose these concepts based on our requirements and motives with minimal code example scenarios.

To generate flexible and maintainable code, it is essential to understand the correct use of inheritance, composition and aggregation concepts.

As a side note, if you are wondering what to choose between inheritance and composition in case both are the options, you need to decide on your requirements and motives. There is no preference for using composition over inheritance because each of them is good for their own purpose.

If you keep these guidelines in mind, it would be easier to decide when to use them to produce quality software.

Here you go with the guidelines to use these concepts.

Inheritance:

You have already read some scenarios with code examples, where the use of inheritance is indispensable, in an earlier question and quick notes i.e. inheritance relationship with an interface and subclasses, similarly, with an abstract class and subclasses.

Here are some more focus points to use the inheritance concept:

If you want to use almost all the functionality of an existing class in your new class, and or maybe want to modify one or two public methods, then you should use inheritance.

For example, you are using all the functionalities of the *Player* class in the *MediaPlayer* class. However, if you wish you can override and define any functionality of the *Player* class in the *MediaPlayer*. As an example, you may not like the codec functionality of the *Player* class and wish to implement a brand-new codec in the *MediaPlayer* class.

```java
//Base class
class Player {
    public void play() {
    }

    public void pause() {
    }

    public void stop() {
    }

    public void codec() {
    }
}
// Child class
class MediaPlayer extends Player {

    public void files() {
    }
}
```

Besides this, you need to consider that the subclass is a proper subtype of the super class. In the above example, the *MediaPlayer* class is a proper subtype of the *Player* class. They are in the same logical domain.

Consider other examples - the Dog and Cat are a subtype of Animal. In other words, the subclass should follow IS-A relationship with super class, e.g. Dog IS-A animal, Cat IS-A animal. Similarly, in the above-given example, the Media Player IS-A Player.

Composition and aggregation:

If you think that there is a HAS-A relationship (Room HAS-A window, Car HAS-A driver, etc.) between parent and child objects, then you should use composition and aggregation.

If the parent object should own the lifespan of composed child objects, then use composition e.g. Room HAS-A window and Room HAS-A door. If the parent object does not own the child's life, then use aggregation e.g. Car HAS-A driver.

So, as a focus point, check for HAS-A relationship between parent and child classes and their life ownership to choose composition and aggregation.

Let's model classes for a simple scenario using inheritance, composition and aggregation concepts for more clarity.

Consider a simple scenario in which a car has an engine, a chassis, and a driver. The Engine must have a start and stop operations and the driver will drive the car. That's it.

Assumption:

✓ The driver and chassis of the car do not have different types.

✓ The engine can be of different types such as a petrol engine, diesel engine, and gas engine, etc.

Let's design the classes for them, and see when the composition or aggregation or inheritance can be a good choice based on our motive?

Driver & Chassis class:

First, let's model the *Driver* and *Chassis* classes. The *Driver* and *Chassis* class do not have different types such as smart driver and experience driver etc. or some special type of chassis. So, they should be an individual class.

```java
class Driver {

    public void drive() {
        System.out.println("Drive...");
    }
}

class Chassis {

    public void setChassis() {
        System.out.println("Chassis...");
    }
}
```

Engine Class:

The engine is of different types such as a petrol engine, diesel engine, and gas engine, etc. according to the given scenario.

We see that all types of engines are a proper subtype of an engine and they follow the IS-A relationship e.g. petrol engine IS-A engine. So, we can use inheritance relationships here.

Secondly, it is mentioned that an engine must have a start and stop operations, so, we can make the engine as an interface with contracts start and stop.

All subclasses i.e. petrol engine and gas engine will implement the engine interface. The code will look like as given here.

```java
interface Engine {

    void start();

    void stop();
}

class PetrolEngine implements Engine {

    @Override
    public void start() {

    }

    @Override
    public void stop() {

    }
}

class DieselEngine implements Engine {

    @Override
    public void start() {

    }

    @Override
    public void stop() {

    }
}

class GasEngine implements Engine {
```

```
        @Override
        public void start() {

        }

        @Override
        public void stop() {

        }
}
```

So far, we designed the *Driver*, *Chassis* and *Engine* class. Now, let's go to the *Car* class.

As in the given scenario, a car has an engine, chassis, and driver. If we look closely, they are following HAS-A relationship i.e. Car HAS-A engine, Car HAS-A chassis, and Car HAS-A driver. So, we can compose all these classes into the Car class as shown below.

```
class Car {
        //class fields
        Chassis chassis;
        Engine engine;
        Driver driver;
}
```

Now, we need to decide on which objects we need to use the composition concept and for which to aggregation.

Logically, on the destruction of the *Car* object, the *Chassis* object should be destroyed, and the *Engine* and the *Driver* objects should not be destroyed.

In other words, the *Car* object must hold the life cycle of the *Chassis* object, but not of the *Engine* and the *Driver* objects.

So, the composition will be used with the *Chassis* class and the aggregation with the *Engine* and the *Driver* class.

We can create an object of the *Chassis* class inside the constructor, and we can receive the objects of the *Engine* and the *Driver* from outside the *Car* class as shown below.

```
class Car {
        Chassis chassis;
        Engine engine;
        Driver driver;

        public Car(Engine engine, Driver driver) {
                this.chassis = new Chassis();
                this.engine = engine;
                this.driver = driver;

        }
}
```

Here are more points that help choose inheritance and composition.

✓ In the case of multiple inheritance using classes, the composition is only the option. The languages such as Java and C# do not support multiple inheritance like C++. In other words, a class cannot inherit multiple classes but single only. In that case, composition and aggregation play an important role.

✓ There may be a situation where you find that the Inheritance is tightly coupled, whereas the composition is not as you read in the answer to previous question # 24.

About the Author

The author is a highly experienced software professional and passionate about designing and developing quality software.

He is also a coding lover and expertise in OOP concepts besides multiple programming languages such as C, C++, Java, and C# and has been coding for decades.

He is a technical blogger and manages his blog on https://www.interviewsansar.com website to share his skills with the world.